G. D. H. COLE:
SELECTED WORKS

PRACTICAL ECONOMICS

PRACTICAL ECONOMICS
or
Studies in Economic Planning

G. D. H. COLE

Volume 8

LONDON AND NEW YORK

First published 1937 by Routledge

2 Park Square, Milton Park, Abingdon, Oxfordshire OX14 4RN
711 Third Avenue, New York, NY 10017

Routledge is an imprint of the Taylor & Francis Group, an informa business

First issued in paperback 2017

Copyright © 1937 H A Cole

All rights reserved. No part of this book may be reprinted or reproduced or utilised in any form or by any electronic, mechanical, or other means, now known or hereafter invented, including photocopying and recording, or in any information storage or retrieval system, without permission in writing from the publishers.

Notice:
Product or corporate names may be trademarks or registered trademarks, and are used only for identification and explanation without intent to infringe.

British Library Cataloguing in Publication Data
A catalogue record for this book is available from the British Library

ISBN 13: 978-0-415-56651-3 (Set)
ISBN 13: 978-0-415-59840-8 (Volume 8) (hbk)
ISBN 13: 978-1-138-56283-7 (Volume 8) (pbk)

Publisher's Note
The publisher has gone to great lengths to ensure the quality of this reprint but points out that some imperfections in the original copies may be apparent.

Disclaimer
The publisher has made every effort to trace copyright holders and would welcome correspondence from those they have been unable to trace.

PRACTICAL ECONOMICS
OR
STUDIES IN ECONOMIC PLANNING

BY
G. D. H. COLE

First published (Pelican Books) 1937

MADE AND PRINTED IN GREAT BRITAIN FOR PENGUIN BOOKS LIMITED
BY PURNELL AND SONS, LTD. PAULTON (SOMERSET) AND LONDON

CONTENTS

CHAPTER		PAGE
I.	THE ESSENTIALS OF PLANNING . .	7
II.	SOCIALIST PLANNING—THE U.S.S.R. .	41
III.	FASCIST 'PLANNING'—GERMANY AND ITALY	91
IV.	AMERICAN 'PLANNING'—THE NEW DEAL.	137
V.	CAPITALIST 'PLANNING' IN GREAT BRITAIN	218
VI.	CONCLUSION	249

LIST OF CHARTS AND TABLES

	PAGE
ECONOMIC ACTIVITY IN THE U.S.S.R. (*Chart*) .	44
(*Table*) .	45
ECONOMIC ACTIVITY IN GERMANY (*Chart*) .	94
(*Table*) .	95
ECONOMIC ACTIVITY IN ITALY (*Chart*) . .	128
(*Table*) . .	129
ECONOMIC ACTIVITY IN THE UNITED STATES (*Chart*)	140
(*Table*)	141
ECONOMIC ACTIVITY IN GREAT BRITAIN (*Chart*)	220
(*Table*)	221

PRACTICAL ECONOMICS

CHAPTER I

THE ESSENTIALS OF PLANNING

OUR grandfathers believed, with the unquestioning certainty of a religious faith, in *laissez-faire*. They held that, in economic matters, the State had only to keep out of the ring in order to ensure the best results. 'Private enterprise' would do all that was needed. Competition would ensure that consumers would be able to buy goods and services at the cheapest possible rates, and that full advantage would be taken of improving technical methods of production. The employer who charged more than the minimum price, or tried to carry on with obsolete methods, would go speedily to the wall. Only the fittest would survive. Moreover, competition would set the inventors and scientists busily to work devising new methods, so that science would flourish most greatly under the stimulus of the profit motive. Each person, in seeking his own economic interest, would be providentially furthering the interest of all. The search for profit would result in maximum production, because competition would keep profit down to the minimum needed to encourage enterprise, and would compel every profit-seeker to make himself as efficient a servant of the consumers as he possibly could.

In these days, that simple faith has been eclipsed. Our fathers were much less certain of it than our grandfathers; and in our own day it is held at all only by way of obstinate reaction against the prevailing conditions. Some economists continue to preach the theoretical soundness of the older doctrine; but even they have to admit that the chance of seeing it applied in the modern world, as it was largely applied in Victorian England, has become very small indeed.

The *laissez-faire* doctrine was always essentially capitalist in its outlook. It was conceived in terms of a number of private employers, each possessing certain instruments of production and a certain capacity to employ labour. It took the private ownership of capital for granted. Indeed, while it demanded that the State should as far as possible abstain from all interference in economic matters, there was one form of State intervention which it regarded as so axiomatic as not to constitute any interference at all. It looked to the State to uphold the 'rights of property'; for on the inviolability of these rights the power of 'private enterprise' to do its beneficent work was believed to depend.

This form of State intervention was held, under *laissez-faire* principles, to involve that the right to acquire property should be open to all. Capital—that is, property in the means of production—was represented as the result of 'abstinence.' The capitalist was simply the individual who had refrained in the past from living up to his income—or of course, his heir, for inheritance was also taken for granted. The man without property, the wage-earner, was simply the person who had been improvident enough not to save, or, when it was admitted that his earnings were too low for saving to be possible, the person whose productive capacity was too small to make him worthy to join the capitalist class. Moral or economic shortcomings kept him where he was; and the fact of his exclusion from the class of property-owners was therefore no detriment to the justice of the economic system, which rewarded all men perfectly according to their deeds. The system handed out rewards for productive service in the form of wages and the profits of the active employers; and it handed out rewards for the moral service of 'abstinence'—the second great economic virtue—in the form of interest on invested capital. Rent, indeed, was always rather difficult to fit into this scheme of things; for land, unlike capital, could hardly be regarded as the product of abstinence. The earlier classical economists had on this ground something of a prejudice against the landlord. But their successors sloughed it off by regarding land more and more as a form of capital, interchangeable by purchase and sale with other forms, and by dwelling more and more on the part played by capital, and therefore by abstinence, in improving the value of land.

In the early days of modern industrialism, this view of the capitalist as the 'abstinent man' had far more plausibility than it has to-day. Many of the early industrialists did rise from almost nothing, making good by their own enterprise and gradually increasing the scale of their operations by ploughing back their profits into the business instead of expanding their own consumption at an equal rate with their incomes. Some men do rise from the ranks in this way even to-day, far enough to become capitalists on a petty scale. But in these days of joint stock enterprise, no man, however talented or abstinent, gets far merely by saving out of his income. In order to 'go big,' he must get persons already in possession of large capital to back his schemes. Our self-made millionaires have been made, not by personal abstinence, but by their ability to get command of capital owned by others.

Early machine capitalism, in the rising industries of the first half of the nineteenth century, was highly competitive. There were many rival firms, each producing only a small fraction of the total output, and each trying to capture as much of the market as it could. Prices were determined by competition;

and each manufacturer had to make himself efficient enough to compete with his rivals, on penalty of losing his market. Prices did tend to fall as productive efficiency increased; and restriction of output in order to maintain prices was in most cases out of the question. To this extent, the consumers did benefit, and the system did promote maximum production. It was under these conditions, applying to the most important and rapidly growing industries, that the doctrine of *laissez-faire* came to be widely accepted as embodying a universal economic truth.

But as the scale of production increased, until in many industries it became impossible for an employer to start business economically in a small way, and then gradually expand his scale of operations, conditions became very different. In one industry after another, the situation of perfect competition between a large number of rival firms ceased to exist. In certain new industries, of which railways are an outstanding example, it never could exist. For it was manifestly wasteful to build several competing railways to carry goods and passengers between two neighbouring towns when one railway could do all that was needed at less capital cost and with smaller running expenses. The supply of gas and that of water were other early instances in which monopoly, and not competition, seemed clearly to make possible the provision of services at the lowest cost.

Monopoly, however, while it might reduce the cost of supplying a service, gave no guarantee that the consumers would benefit by the lower cost. The monopolist, if he was let alone, could charge what he liked; and his price policy would be settled, not by competitive necessity, but by the elasticity of demand for his particular product in conjunction with the variations of his costs at different levels of output. It might pay him, in exceptional cases, where demand was very elastic and his commodity was produced under conditions of diminishing cost as output increased, to sell at the lowest possible price. But this would not necessarily, or even commonly, be the case. In most instances, the price that would give the monopolist the highest profit would be a higher price than the minimum at which it would pay him to produce.

This being evident, the case for *laissez-faire* in these particular instances, went by the board. Hesitantly, because it seemed dangerous to admit exceptions to the general freedom of 'private enterprise,' the necessity for some form of public regulation was admitted in the case of monopolies. But the exceptions were kept within the narrowest possible limits; and even within these limits as little regulation as possible was actually enforced.

But next, with the further growth of technique, there arose a situation in which, short of actual monopoly, the necessary scale of production became so large that there was room in the market for only a very few firms, and the entry of fresh competitors became very difficult, because the new entrant could not begin in a small scale and work his way up, but must from the start invest a huge capital in order to produce at all. Where such conditions exist, it becomes easy for the few competitors, if they so desire, to confer together, and to establish what is in effect a monopoly by agreeing upon the prices at which they will sell, and perhaps also about the quantities and varieties of goods that they will place on the market. The cartel, with more or less developed common selling agreements, is the most systematic form of this secondary type of monopoly; but, short of the cartel, it can be found in less formal price-fixing and similar arrangements in many branches of modern industry, and on both a national and an international scale.

The advocates of *laissez-faire*, faced with this type of monopoly, hesitated what to do. In the United States, the attempt was made, with singular lack of success, to outlaw it by prohibiting all arrangements for price-fixing between businesses, and by ordering the actual dissolution of trusts and combines held to be contrary to the public interest. In Germany, on the other hand, where the notions of economic individualism were never so strongly held, the State sought to control this type of monopoly by regulating the prices which it was allowed to charge, and by establishing some degree of public supervision. Finally, in Great Britain, it was allowed to grow practically unchecked, but did, in fact, grow less rapidly than in either Germany or America until recent years, probably because British industry was producing more extensively for a diversified world market, and free trade seemed in part to protect the home consumers against restrictive policies or high prices enforced by the combines.

It became, however, increasingly apparent that, under conditions of large-scale production, the capitalist system was very far from guaranteeing to the consumers maximum production at minimum prices. It also became apparent that another assumption of the *laissez-faire* doctrine was not being fulfilled. It had been assumed that, just as employers would all have to sell their goods at the lowest price, so would labourers, competing for jobs, be compelled to sell their labour cheap enough to make it worth while for the employers to employ them all. It was assumed, in fact, that unemployment, save as a comparatively unimportant effect of unavoidable friction in changing over from job to job, would not exist.

But it became plain that in reality unemployment, on a much more serious scale than this, could and did exist. Economists often took refuge in blaming the Trade Unions for maintaining wages at an uneconomic height—that is, at too high a level to make it profitable for employers to engage all the available labour. For a time this explanation was widely accepted; but it was gradually realised that there might in truth be no wage-level at which employers would be prepared to engage all those who were ready to work. This might be the case because the lowering of wages would at the same time lower purchasing power, and so narrow the market for consumers' goods. It was attempted to argue that any such decline would be offset by an increased demand for capital goods, arising out of the higher profits made possible by the lower wages. But the answer to this is that, as capital goods are, in the last resort, useful only for making consumers' goods, the demand for capital goods must depend on the prospective demand for consumers' goods. It was then argued that the lower wages would not, in fact, decrease purchasing power, because prices would fall to a corresponding extent. But, if prices did fall to this extent, there could be no inducement to the employer to engage more labour; for this inducement depends, not on the level of costs alone, but on the relation between costs and selling prices. Finally, it was argued that, as more workers would be employed, as much or more would be paid out in wages as before, despite the lower wage-rates. This, however, is to assume the very thing that is to be proved—that more workers would actually find employment.

In truth, wherever competition is so limited that firms are able to choose their own level of output or price—the two of course going together—there can be no assurance of either maximum production or minimum price, or of full employment of the available supply of labour. *Laissez-faire* no longer offers, even in theory, the prospect of maximum economic advantage.

Nor is this all. As technique advances, the differentiation of products, as well as the necessary scale of production, increases. But each producer of a differentiated product—an Austin car as against a Morris for example, or one patent breakfast food as against another—is in a position of partial, though still competitive, monopoly. Indeed, competition among the rival monopolists can be exceedingly keen; for, in face of a limited total market, each wants to sell as much as he can in order to get the full advantages of the economy of mass-production. But whereas, when products are relatively undifferentiated, this competition can be carried on only in terms of price, it is conducted under conditions of monopolistic competition largely by means of advertisement of the rival branded and patented products. Thus advertisement comes, in many cases, to involve a substantial addition to the costs of production; and yet no firm can afford to dispense with it because, in face of the advertising tactics of its rivals, it will not be able to make the existence or merits of its wares known to the consumers, even if it is offering goods of equal quality at a lower price.

When a number of rival monopolists are competing in this way, the costs of production are artificially inflated; for each firm is prevented by its rivals from taking full advantage of the economies of mass-production, and the costs of advertisement have to be added on to the unnecessarily high costs of manufacture. Moreover, the patent laws, whereby each firm acquires a monopoly for certain gadgets or processes against its rivals, prevent the consumer from getting the best possible article, as this would involve the pooling of the various patents. Where, in order to remedy these defects, the rival producers do combine, the consumer is merely faced with a complete monopoly, and it is not by any means assured that the benefits of cheaper production will be passed on to him in lower prices.

Side by side with these developments of monopoly in its various forms in the field of manufacture, there appears a strong tendency towards the increase of distributive costs. This takes two main forms. In retail distribution, the principal defect is that costs tend to be inflated by excess of competition. For, whereas in the field of manufacture it becomes increasingly difficult for the small-scale business to exist at all, in many branches of retail trade it continues to be relatively easy to make a start with very little capital. This induces a very large number of persons to enter retail trade, attracted by the possibility of working 'on their own' and escaping from the discipline of wage-earning employment. The rate of mortality among these small-scale traders is high; but there are always plenty of new entrants ready to take the places of those who fail. Inevitably, the existence of a large number of redundant retailers raises the level of costs; for each has to accept less trade than he could economically handle. The resulting wastes are very considerable indeed; and for these the consumer has mainly to pay, though a part falls on the unsuccessful retailers, who either lose their small capital and fail, or carry on at a very low level of remuneration for themselves and their invested capital.

But why, it may be asked, are not these high-cost small retailers destroyed by the competition of the larger capitalist firms? Partly because the small retailer offers forms of service—credit to poor purchasers, immediate delivery, the nearness of his little shop to the purchasers' house; and so on—which the large store in many cases does not supply; and partly because the costs of the large stores, which are in active competition with one another, are inflated by the expenses of advertisement. Moreover, the small retailer, having sunk his savings in his shop, is often prepared to carry on at a very low rate of return until his scanty capital and credit are exhausted.

Retail trade, then, is very wastefully conducted from the standpoint of the consumer. But wholesale trade is no more immune from criticism. Goods, on their way from the producer to the consumer, often pass through an unnecessary number of hands. In addition, wholesaling, which demands a relatively large capital, lends itself easily to monopolistic arrangements among the firms engaged in a particular branch of trade. By restricting sales through high prices, the wholesaler can often increase his bargaining power against the producers, who scramble the more to sell him their wares the smaller the quantity he is ready to buy. This enables the wholesaler to buy most cheaply when he needs least to sell, or in other words when he charges a high price to the final retailer. His margin of profit is thus apt to be larger on a small than on a big turnover. Nowhere is monopoly more dangerous than in wholesale distribution; for the distributor, unlike the manufacturer, tends to be faced with rising costs as turnover is increased.

In face of all these restrictive conditions, it is no longer possible to contend that *laissez-faire* offers any assurance of high output or low prices to the consumers. On the contrary, it seems to involve more and more evident wastes. These wastes occur both where production and distribution remain in the hands of numerous competing firms, and where this sort of competition is replaced by complete or partial capitalist monopoly. For in the former case the economies of large-scale production are to a great extent lost; and these economies are of ever-increasing importance under modern technical conditions. And, where monopoly tends to replace competition, it is apt to prefer restriction to plenty, because the highest profit can be secured by limiting supplies in order to maintain prices. Moreover, over a large part of the field, advertising expenses swallow up a considerable part of the saving in costs of production made possible by improving technique.

Under these circumstances, the demand for a planned economy steadily gains force. Planning, under public auspices, and with a view to the satisfaction of the consumers' needs, offers the prospect of eliminating the wastes inherent in unregulated competition, whether of the older or of the newer monopolistic variety; and it also affords the means, in industries already under large-scale monopolistic control, of substituting a policy of plenty and cheapness for one of scarcity based on high prices and profits. The old *laissez-faire* doctrines, in effect, reckoned without two forces which have come to be of paramount importance under modern conditions—the economy of large-scale production, including a complete pooling of patent rights and an elimination of the costs of competitive advertisement, and the existence in many industries of conditions necessarily leading to monopoly, so that the alternatives are no longer State regulation and free competition, but planning under restrictive capitalist control and planning under public auspices, with a view to the maximum satisfaction of the consumers' needs.

The conception of a 'planned economy' remains, however, so far vague and ambiguous. For some would-be planners envisage 'planning' primarily as a conferment of regulative power over each industry on some organisation representing the capitalist businesses engaged in it, under no more than a very general control exercised by the State in the general interest; while others insist that planning involves not merely the separate organisation of each industry into a co-operating group, but a right adjustment between industries and a social direction of the distribution of labour and capital between alternative uses. One set of planners, again, regards planning as a means of so reorganising capitalism as to give it a new lease of life; while another looks to it as a means of replacing capitalism by social ownership and operation of industry.

Now clearly the conception of planning as meaning merely the bringing of each industry under the control of a common authority representative of the capitalist firms engaged in it is in effect a proposal for the generalisation of capitalist monopoly. For the natural inclination of authorities thus constituted must be to pursue the restrictive policies associated with capitalist monopolies as they now exist. It is indeed usually proposed that the working of this system of compulsory monopoly should be made subject to some sort of collective control. But this only brings us face to face once more with the difficulties of making such controls effective from the consumers' point of view—difficulties which have been amply illustrated by the history of past and present monopolies and, more especially, of such compulsory monopolies as the agricultural Marketing Boards and the regulative agencies under the Coal Mines Act of 1930. If scarcity pays the monopolist better than plenty, it is not easy for the State to compel him to pursue plenty, as long as it leaves him to conduct the actual business—especially if the State itself is largely dominated by the influence of the monopolists. Planning, in this sense, instead of making goods cheaper for the consumers, is apt to put the authority of the State behind policies designed to make them dear —as it has actually done under the Coal Mines Act and in the various schemes of agricultural marketing.

It is sometimes argued that this would not occur

if planning of this type were generalised, and a common council of all the capitalist planners set up to co-ordinate their activities. For in that case, it is argued, each group would be alert to correct the anti-social policies of the others. But it is surely far more probable that all the leading groups would join together to exploit the public, on principles generally agreed. Honour among monopolists would lead to mutual endorsement of restrictive policies, as long as these did not pass certain limits of extortion. There would be no substitution of the principle of plenty for that of scarcity conducive to maximum profit.

Planning, if it is to involve any real unleashing of the forces of production, must be controlled by an authority aiming at plenty, rather than by one dominated by the notion of producers' profit. But this means that planning must involve disinterested operation of industry, and not merely an external public control; for all experience goes to show that it is impracticable to impose a policy on industry from outside. If plenty is to be secured, plenty must be the object of those who are actually administering the machine; for the actual administrators are bound to be decisive in settling the policy which is to be pursued.

Planning, then, if it is to be effective in securing plenty, turns out to involve disinterested, or rather consumer-interested, management. It involves either

State operation of industry, or at all events operation by persons whose concern is with public service rather than private profit. This, however, strikes at the very roots of 'private enterprise.' It requires some form of 'socialism,' at any rate in the administrative sense, even if the administration of industry is to be entrusted, not to the State, but rather to special *ad hoc* boards, or commissions of impartial administrators appointed under the State's authority.

But there is a further requirement—that planning shall proceed, not within each industry or service regarded as a perfectly self-contained unit, but with the object of securing the best possible allocation of the available productive resources to different activities, and therewith the fullest possible satisfaction of the consumers' needs. If each industry is organised separately as a unit, wasteful competition will only be transferred to a higher plane. The Gas Board will be wasting resources in trying to induce consumers to use more gas, while the Electricity Board is hard at them to use more electricity. Each controlling agency will be seeking to maximise the consumption of its own wares, irrespective of the repercussions upon other industries.

This is apt to be the consequence of piecemeal planning, as it is already practised in certain services. But it is clearly unsatisfactory. It involves

THE ESSENTIALS OF PLANNING 25

many of the same wastes as arise under conditions of 'monopolistic competition' where industries are privately owned and controlled. Maximum satisfaction of the consumers' needs involves inter-industrial planning, not the mere unification of each industry as a separate unit.

Planning of this comprehensive sort is fully consistent with the division of responsibility between distinct administrative authorities for each separate industry. But it means that each *ad hoc* industrial authority must work to a general programme laid down by some co-ordinating authority for industry as a whole. It involves, in other words, some sort of National Economic Plan such as exists to-day in Soviet Russia, and nowhere else in the world.

But, as soon as the idea of such a comprehensive Plan is accepted, other considerations arise. Capitalism accepts, and works in relation to, the distribution of incomes which it finds actually in being. It produces for a market which it takes, broadly, for granted. Each capitalist producer, or group of producers, tries to swing demand his way. But he assumes that, if consumers spend more on his goods, they will have less to spend on the products of other industries. He takes the income structure of the community as it is.

As fast as capitalist production for profit comes to be replaced by publicly controlled production, new standards of valuation come into play. A State attempting to plan industry in the general interest cannot take the existing structure of consumers' demand as a postulate: it has to consider whether a different structure of demand would contribute to a higher standard of social welfare. It has to consider *needs*, and not merely demands arising out of the existing distribution of incomes.

As soon, however, as needs come to be considered, the distribution of incomes comes itself under criticism. Up to a certain point, it is possible for the State to leave the original distribution of incomes as it was, but to modify its effects by redistributive taxation, of which the proceeds can then be applied to the financing of social services. The State can in this way supply the poorer consumers with certain services either free, as in the case of elementary education, or at a reduced price, as in that of subsidised housing. Or it can pay out sums derived from taxation as incomes to the aged, or the unemployed, or the sick, and leave the recipients to spend the money as they think best. In modern times, the State has made increasing use of both these methods, though there has been at the same time a tendency so to adjust the tax-system as to place part of the cost of social services upon the poor—by higher indirect taxation for example, or by exacting compulsory contributions under social insurance schemes.

The State can also, within certain limits, modify the original distribution of incomes, apart from taxation, by prescribing minimum wage-rates. But this method, which is usually applied only to industries in which wages are held to be abnormally low, cannot be carried at all far under the capitalist system, largely because of the international complications which it is certain to involve.

For if wages are raised in certain industries above the level they would reach in the absence of State regulation, the effect is apt to be a reduction of the numbers employed in these industries. This need not be the case, where the higher wages lead to the reorganisation of the industries concerned on more efficient lines, as actually happened to a considerable extent when the Trade Board system was introduced. But where an industry is already being carried on with ordinary efficiency, the enforcement of higher wages is likely in most cases to reduce the willingness of the firms in it to employ labour. In any case wages cannot be much increased, in some industries as against others, without causing a shift of demand from the industries in which the increases have occurred to those in which they have not—or, of course, a diversion of demand from home to foreign products.

If wages were increased simultaneously in all industries, the effects would be somewhat different. The possibility of a diversion of demand to imported products would remain, but this would occur, over industry as a whole, only if the foreign exchanges were prevented from adjusting themselves to the changed relation between home and foreign costs. Given adjustable exchange rates, the effect would be principally to shift demand away from those industries in which labour cost formed a large part of total cost of production towards those in which labour cost was a smaller part of the total. This might carry with it some readjustment of imports and exports, the latter group of industries increasing, and the former decreasing its exports, while the reverse would be true of imports.

What matters to us here is that any considerable attempt by the State to raise wages by law is likely, under the gold or any fixed exchange standard, to increase imports and reduce exports, and therewith to contract profits and employment. It will therefore be strongly opposed. This does not hold good under a system of adjustable exchange rates; but even so the effect is to re-distribute demand between different types of goods and services, raising profits and employment in some industries and lowering them in others. This means that there will be strong opposition to such a policy from the industries likely to be affected adversely. Nor does it at all follow that the result of the changes will be to benefit the industries of whose products it is desirable, for social reasons, to increase the consumption.

The compulsory increases in wages will, of course, have other effects as well. As selling prices will not need to rise in the same proportion as wages—non-wage costs remaining as before—there will be, if total employment remains the same, a rise in the total real income in the hands of the wage-earners, at the expense of the incomes represented by non-wage costs, *e.g.*, those of the recipients of rent and interest and profits. This again will cause a shift in demand, but in this case the shift will be definitely good from the social standpoint, because it will be on the whole a transfer of demand from richer to poorer persons.

This effect, however, may not be produced if the rise in wages reduces the volume of employment by diverting activity to forms of production in which more capital and less labour is employed. When wages rise, capital will become for the moment relatively cheap, and there will be some impetus given to the mechanisation of industry. This will cause a larger demand for capital. But the fall of non-wage incomes will tend to reduce the supply of savings, and therewith to raise the rates of interest demanded by lenders of capital. The higher interest rates will thereupon have two effects. They will cause a rise in non-wage costs, which will be reflected in higher prices, and will thus cancel a part of the advantage of the higher wages in terms of real purchasing power. And they will also do away with the relative dearness of labour, by making capital dearer as well, and thus check both the impetus towards mechanisation and the shift from industries using a larger to those using a smaller proportion of labour in production.

Thus States under capitalism can do only a little to raise wages without reducing employment, and can do hardly anything unless the foreign exchanges are left free to adjust themselves to the changed level of costs.[1] Moreover, even under an adjustable exchange system, the effect of the higher wages will be liable to be, in the short run, a reduction in employment through mechanisation and, in the long run, a rise in selling prices, which will take back most, if not all, of the real advantage conferred on the wage-earners by the change.

In view of all these complications, States, under the capitalist system, are likely to be very reluctant to make any extensive use of their power to raise wages. The only country which has followed this wage-raising policy over an extensive field is Australia, where, as wages rose, tariffs were put up to keep out the imports which would otherwise have come in. This enabled the industrial workers to get higher incomes at the expense of the farmers, who

---

[1] They can, indeed, act under a fixed exchange system if they are prepared to raise tariffs high enough to keep out the imports that would otherwise come in. This was done in Australia when the minimum wage system was extensively used for raising wages after its first introduction.

had to pay more for their requirements of industrial goods without being able to sell their agricultural goods at higher prices in export markets. The farmers' opposition therefore set limits to the height to which wages could be raised; but within these limits the industrial workers did get higher real wages. In such a country as Great Britain, however, the very different balance between industrial and agricultural production would prevent this result from being achieved.

In face of difficulties of this order, 'progressive' Governments which set out to increase the real incomes of the poorer classes are impelled to proceed much more by extending the social services than by raising wages. Here too, however, there are powerful obstacles to be met. It requires a very strong Government to raise taxation levied on the rich enough to make any substantial difference in the class-distribution of incomes. For, under capitalism, it is the capitalist who has to provide employment; and the amount of employment he is willing to provide depends on the degree of confidence which he feels in the prospect of profit. His confidence, however, is apt to be reduced when he finds himself confronted with what he regards as a 'confiscatory' Government. He is apt to employ less labour, and thereby to destroy fully as much purchasing power as the Government's measures have conferred on the poorer classes.

It is in fact very difficult to alter materially, under capitalism, the distribution of incomes which arises out of the unrestricted working of the profit system. If the State wants to alter the distribution of incomes a great deal, so as to bring production much closer to its conception of real social needs, it soon finds itself under the necessity of changing the economic system instead of merely tinkering with it. It discovers that capitalism cannot be made to serve the real needs of the people; and it either gives up the attempt to get real needs satisfied, or goes on to a frontal onslaught upon capitalism itself. For it becomes plain that, if capitalism is abolished and replaced by a planned system of production under collective control, there will be no limit to the extent to which real needs can be met, short of the absolute limit set by the extent of the community's productive power.

Let us suppose that capitalism has been abolished, and collectively planned production under social ownership has been substituted for it. What, then, is the situation? The community possesses certain productive resources, all of which it means to use in meeting what it considers the most urgent needs. It therefore proceeds directly to allocate these resources to the various forms of production which it considers most important.

What happens next? It would be possible for the State, instead of paying anybody an income in money, simply to ration the goods and services among its citizens in accordance with its collective estimate of their respective needs. It may in fact do this in the case of a substantial number of goods and services; but it is unlikely to do it with the majority. For, though there are certain elementary needs which everyone shares, outside this range of needs what people want most is largely a matter of temperament. When once the elementary common needs have been met, human needs have not been fully satisfied; but the next great need is to be allowed the power of choice. Everyone needs moderate luxuries as well as sheer necessaries; but everyone's need is not for the same luxuries.

Accordingly, if everyone cannot have as much of everything as he would like to have if he could have it for nothing—and we may take it for granted that everyone cannot—the sensible course is to put prices on things, and let people buy what they want most. They can, however, buy only what is on the market—that is, what the planned economy chooses to supply.

But a planned economy, planned with the object of satisfying human needs, will aim first of all at satisfying the basic human needs, and thereafter, up to the limit of the available productive resource, at giving people what they want—subject, of course, to the power to refuse supply of definitely noxious goods, such as opium, or to make artificially dear goods of which, short of entire prohibition, it wishes to discourage the use. The resources of production, beyond those employed in meeting basic needs—and of course those required for the maintenance and increase of capital—will therefore be directed to giving the consumers what they want.

But what will the consumers want? The demands made by the consumers depend largely on their incomes; or, in other words, the total structure of demand is largely determined by the way in which incomes are distributed in the community. The State, beyond insisting on an adequate standard of nutrition, clothing, housing and education, and discouraging noxious forms of consumption, need not concern itself with the tastes of its citizens. It has no preference of its own for supplying one thing rather than another. But it is concerned that what it supplies shall give as much satisfaction as possible; and it is accordingly concerned to promote as near an approach to equality of consuming power as is consistent with getting production efficiently carried on.

In practice this means, in the earlier stages of a planned economy, three things. It means the liquidation, as speedily as possible, of the forms of income which arise not from personal service, but from the possession of property in the means of production or of claims based on the investment or loan of capital. It means, secondly, the provision for all citizens of a minimum income, in goods or in money or in both, sufficient to supply the basic needs of life. And it means, thirdly, the sharing out of the remaining products as nearly as possible in proportion to the value of the personal services rendered by the various producers, but subject to a maximum limit designed to prevent the re-emergence of economic class-distinctions in a new form.

This is not a theoretically ideal distribution of income: it is the best practical distribution obtainable in the earlier stages of the working of a planned economic system based on public ownership. And it is this form of income distribution which, when it is established, will determine the nature of the demands to which production will have to respond.

Beyond question, a system in which inequality is thus limited will be much easier to plan for than a system in which gross inequalities are allowed to prevail. There will be, under it, no question of leaving any productive resource unused unless it is regarded as economically preferable to scrap it and replace it by a more efficient instrument for the satisfaction of needs and desires. There will be no unemployment save frictional unemployment, which must exist to some extent under any system. All productive resources, including all human agents, will be used to the full, up to the point at which more leisure seems to the common judgment preferable to more goods. Production of useful things will be limited only by backwardness of technique and by the demand for leisure. Within these limits, maximum production will be continually achieved, as it never has been or can be under capitalism, because capitalism makes private profit and not service the controlling factor in deciding whether things are to be produced or not.

So far I have spoken theoretically. But clearly what I have been describing is what actually happens to-day in the Soviet Union. True, the Russian standard of living is still very low—much lower than the standards which exist in advanced capitalist countries. But up to the limits set by productive power the Soviet Union is producing all it can, whereas of no capitalist country can the same be said.

Moreover, the planned system of the Soviet Union begets not only maximum production, but also, within the bounds of practicability, maximum welfare. It not only produces as much as it technically can, but distributes the product as well as it economically can. It is true that, for the present, the need to provide vast masses of new capital for the purpose of industrialising a great backward country must to some extent check the immediate rise in the standard of living—in order to make possible a more rapid rise in the future; and it is true that the need to arm heavily for defence in a war-threatened world also stands in the way of improved social conditions. But the Soviet Union does not condemn its citizens to unnecessary poverty by sheer failure to use the productive resources which lie ready to its hand. This, however, is exactly what the 'free' capitalisms of Great Britain and America habitually do.

But what, it may be asked, of the planned capitalisms of the Fascist States—Germany and Italy? Has not Germany, at any rate, with her 'Plan of National Self-Sufficiency,' come near to abolishing unemployment, and bringing all her productive resources into active play? Yes, in a sense she has. But there is a vital difference. Germany has reduced unemployment very greatly by measures of re-armament and national economic equipment for self-sufficiency in face of war. But whereas the object of full employment in the Soviet Union is to raise the standards of living for the whole people, the object of German employment is to make Germany more formidable in a military sense.

But, it may be said, what does the object matter, as long as full employment, or something not far short of it, is actually secured? It matters a great deal, for two reasons, even apart from the not unimportant reason that the German way disastrously menaces the peace of the world. It matters, first, because the German way of securing full employment, so far from raising, actually lowers the standard of living of the people, both by diverting productive resources into the supplying of military demands and by twisting the whole productive system into inefficiency by causing to be made at home goods which could be far better purchased abroad by exchange. The object of full employment is not full employment, but more production and better distribution of the products to the people. Employment is not an end but a means. It should be a means to welfare: Germany makes it a means to predatory power.

Secondly, the object matters because the German way of reducing unemployment involves huge unproductive expenditure by the State, and threatens the whole economy with collapse the moment this expenditure slackens off. It piles up public debts to create not means to future wealth, unless wealth can be got by sheer brigandage, but things which either produce nothing, such as armaments, or prevent the German economic system from developing in the most productive way. The entire economy becomes adjusted to a depressed standard of living, and dependent on the maintenance of uneconomic demand. It is therefore self-destructive, unless it can sustain itself by brigandage. But one thing clear about modern war is that, economically, it cannot possibly benefit even the victors. International brigandage is not a possible road to national wealth.

In the three studies which follow, an attempt has been made to sum up, very broadly, the outstanding features of three recent—but very different—attempts at planning. The Soviet Union represents planning for human welfare, on a basis of common ownership. The Fascist countries represent planning for war, on a basis which preserves capitalist inequality and even exaggerates it by measures which must lower the workers' standards of life. The United States of America represents—what? Certainly, neither of these, and certainly, in a fundamental sense, not planning at all. The 'New Deal' has never been a plan, or aimed at a planned economy. It has been a series of expedients, designed to see capitalism safely through a bad time, and so arranged as to be as far as possible terminable as soon as the emergency is over.

It may be held, on this ground, that a study of the 'New Deal' is out of place in this book. But it is not. For planning can arise without being itself planned. Expedients adopted in an emergency may so establish themselves as to become irremovable. Planning may emerge, in at least a partial form, without any single comprehensive plan being laid down, or any single comprehensive idea behind it.

Now clearly this is the way in which some sort of planning looks most likely to arise in Great Britain, if it arises at all. We have already in Great Britain our expedients, worked out in face of our special emergencies. We have our Agricultural Marketing Boards, our Coal Mines Acts and the control schemes established under them, our Steel Corporation, our Exchange Equalisation Fund, and a host of other innovations that have at least some appearance of planning in this or that particular field. I have included a study of the 'Roosevelt experiment' because its history throws some light on the working of this sort of pseudo-planning in a capitalist economy in certain respects not unlike our own, and because it provides a telling contrast of method to both the Fascist and the Soviet systems.

Finally, I have added a short chapter dealing with British 'planning.' But this is no more than the merest outline. I would refer readers who want fuller treatment to my *Principles of Economic Planning*, in which the entire problem, in its relation to Great Britain, is discussed at much greater length.

CHAPTER II

SOCIALIST PLANNING—THE U.S.S.R.

ALTHOUGH other countries have introduced in recent years an increasing element of planning into their economic structure, Soviet Russia is, of course, the one country in which any thorough-going attempt to institute a planned economy has been made. We have therefore evidently to take most careful notice of the Russian example; but before we set out to comment upon the achievements of planning in the U.S.S.R. it is important to consider wherein the problem which the Russians have had to face is like and unlike the problems of planning elsewhere—and especially in the more highly industrialised, far wealthier and more educated societies of Western Europe and North America.

There are, obviously, certain outstanding differences. Socialist planning in the U.S.S.R. came as the sequel to war, revolution, civil war, and economic blockade. The old Czarist system, with its remarkable contrasts of large-scale industrialism and exceedingly backward peasant production, collapsed under the strain of war far sooner and more completely than the economic systems of the more advanced belligerent countries. This economic collapse was an important factor in causing military defeat and preparing the way for revolution. But it meant that the revolution inherited, not an economic structure working with its normal degree of efficiency, but only the ruins of the pre-war Russian system. The Bolsheviks took over the control of a country already broken on the wheel of war, and desperately short both of necessaries for immediate consumption and of the means of replenishing its stock by fresh production.

Moreover, in the circumstances which existed for some time after the revolutions of 1917 these conditions were bound to get very much worse. Under Lvov and Kerensky the processes of economic disintegration went on apace; and the Bolsheviks had to face in the early years of their authority continuous civil war complicated by foreign intervention and economic blockade. There were in the country no adequate means of keeping such instruments of production as had survived the chaos in proper repair, or of making new ones; and the Russian Ishmael was in no position to acquire the needed instruments from abroad. The most that could be done was to keep the factories, mines and railways working somehow, with ever-diminishing efficiency as irreplaceable plant wore out or was destroyed, and, for the rest, to rely on the peasants, who had assumed control of the land, to go on producing enough foodstuffs to save the population from sheer decimation by famine.

The problem was made the more intractable because Russia was desperately short of knowledgeable technicians and craftsmen, of administrators of every sort, and of men of experience in the arts of government and economic organisation. As long as the civil wars lasted, what personnel there was had to attend to the tasks of the moment, and all longer-run measures of economic reconstruction had to be postponed. There was, and could be, no economic planning until the fighting was over, and the Communist leaders could pause to take stock of their sorely battered economic resources with some assurance that the country was theirs to re-make after the new pattern of their hopes.

Even then, the first task was to ward off sheer starvation, and long-run plans had still to wait on what was best for averting immediate collapse. In at least one field—that of electrification—Lenin began to plan the instant the war pressure was relaxed; and the choice of electrical power as the gateway to a planned economy was significant of the idea which the Bolsheviks had already in mind. Lenin's plan for the electrical development of all Russia—formulated as early as 1920—is the direct ancestor of the Five-Year Plans. But though in this field a beginning was made at once, for the rest planning had to wait, or rather to be subordinated

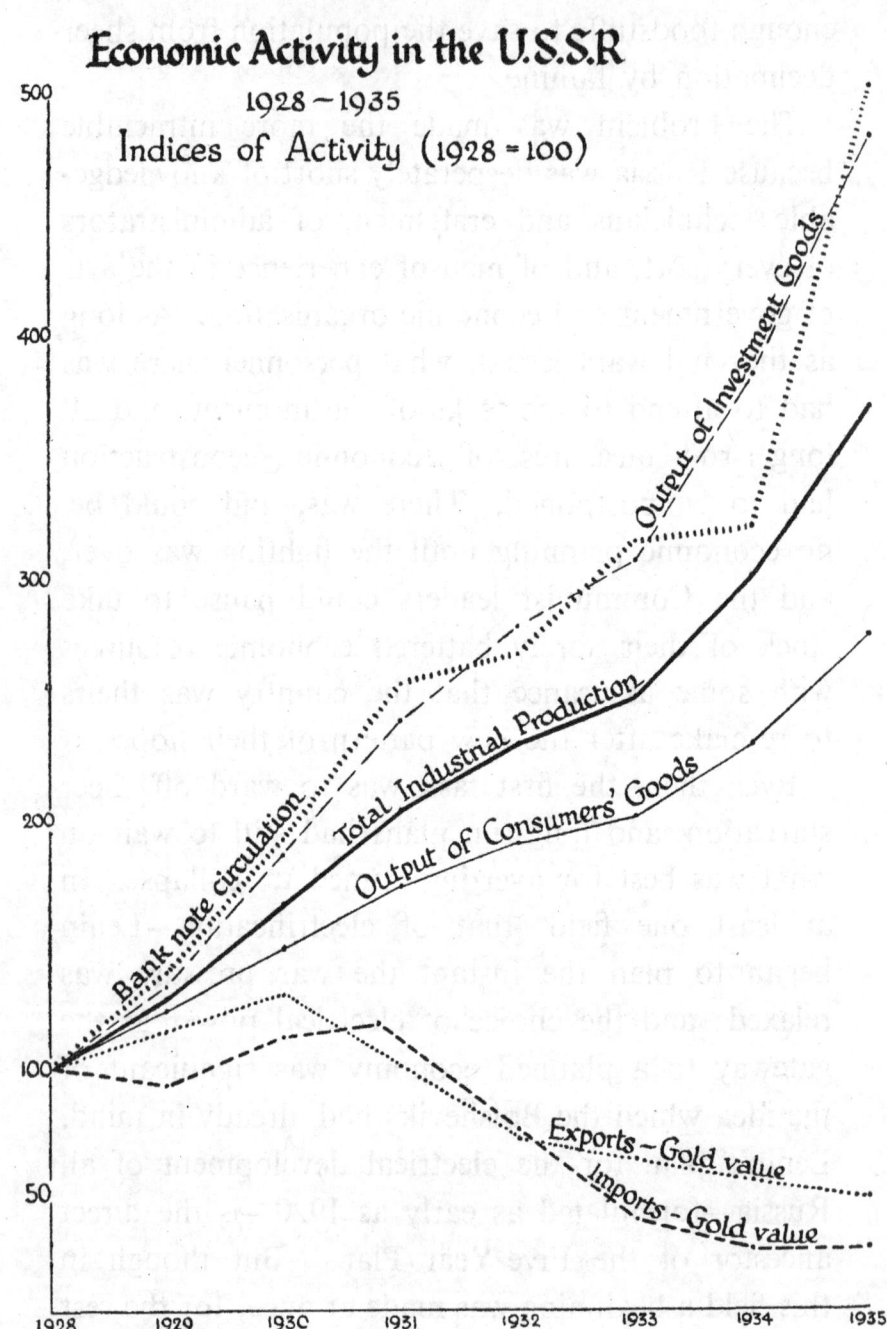

ECONOMIC ACTIVITY IN THE U.S.S.R., 1928–1935
(1928 = 100)

	1929	1930	1931	1932	1933	1934	1935
Industrial Production	126	164	203	231	250	300	369
Output of Investment Goods	131	185	240	279	307	382	481
Output of Consumers' Goods	122	147	172	190	200	230	274
Note Circulation	138	191	255	268	314	321	500 (estd.)
Net Imports—Gold Value	92	111	116	74	37	24	25
Net Exports—Gold Value	114	128	100	71	61	52	45

to the immediate claims of the consumers for as much production as the battered economic system could be somehow patched up to supply.

Accordingly the successor to 'War Communism' was the 'New Economic Policy'—a temporary reversion to the encouragement of planless private trade and production. The N.E.P. was by no means a reversion to Capitalism; for under it most large-scale industry was steadily reorganised under State control and management, and there was a complete public monopoly of foreign trade, together with a co-ordination of most retail trading in the hands of State-controlled Co-operative bodies and State shops. Moreover, the strictness of the Soviet Government's political control was never for a moment relaxed, so that concessions made under the N.E.P. could be at any time modified or revoked, to any extent consistent with the prime necessity of increasing the available supply of elementary products. The N.E.P. did involve temporarily large concessions to the private trader and the small-scale producer and, in these fields, a temporary return to the incentive of profit as a stimulus to production. To a substantial extent, it restored the 'market' and the 'pricing system' as means of getting goods produced and distributed. But throughout these 'capitalist' methods were able to operate only under the shadow of the Communist political power. To the limited extent to

SOCIALIST PLANNING—THE U.S.S.R.

which Capitalism came back, it came only as a tenant-at-will of the Soviet power, and not as an independent holder of economic authority.

The N.E.P. did tide Russia over the immediate crisis and create a situation which made real planning possible. No sooner had this been achieved than Lenin's successors set to work to plan in real earnest. The New Economic Policy made way for the first Five-Year Plan.

There is clearly no reason to suppose that the introduction of planning into any Western country will come about under conditions at all resembling those which have just been described. In the first place it would take not only a war, but civil war as well, to bring such conditions into existence; and secondly only the most prolonged and destructive warfare could reduce the industrial equipment of any advanced country to such chaos as existed in Russia in the early years of the Soviet régime. Industrially, even the most war-shattered productive equipment one can easily imagine in Great Britain or Germany or the United States would possess an immediate power to deliver supplies immeasurably greater than was found in post-war Russia.

On the other hand, in the matter of food supply the Russians possessed a large advantage over Great Britain or Germany, and even some over the United States. The Russians could be starved, according to Western standards; but they could not be positively starved out. Their problem of providing food for the urban population was serious enough; but so large a part of the total population was rural that it was nothing like the problem that would face a more urbanised country confronted with economic collapse. The means of growing food still existed, impaired as they were by the acute shortage of agricultural implements of every sort; and it was possible for Russia, even at the worst, to exist, however barely, upon her domestic supplies of food. There were famines, no doubt; and everywhere the standard of existence was meagre. But there was never the threat of sheer mass-starvation, as it would confront Great Britain if overseas supplies were cut off.

This altered the entire emphasis of the Russian struggle. The industrial part of the N.E.P. was largely an effort to provide industrial goods for supply to the peasants in exchange for the food which they were in a position to produce. In this effort the resources of large-scale production had to be mobilised and improved, so that a partial planning of large-scale industry arose as a by-product of the N.E.P. itself. When, by means of the N.E.P., food supplies had been raised above the point of positive danger to the régime, it became possible to erect, on the foundations laid by this partial plan, a more comprehensive plan for industry as a whole. For a little while, planned industry confronted planless agriculture; but as soon as the basis of industrial planning seemed to be assured, Stalin made haste—undue haste—to extend the sphere of planning to cover agriculture as well. It was not thought possible to plan agricultural output on the same basis of vast-scale production as was being applied to industry under the influence of American ideas. Some huge State farms, such as 'Gigant,' had already been started, mainly on land previously not cultivated at all. But for by far the greater part of Russian agriculture this was recognised to be too great a leap from the primitive to the most advanced; and Stalin contented himself with the 'Collective'—that is, with the co-operative farming group carrying on cultivation for the most part in common, but still preserving some traces of the older systems in some private ownership of beasts and utensils, and sometimes some private cultivation of patches of land attached to the collective farm.

Now, it is quite clear that no such institution as the Russian collective farm could possibly be superposed on the quite different agricultural tradition of any Western country. The *kolkhoz* is the collectivised farm emerging out of a primitive peasant economy which has neither wholly lost nor forgotten the collective characteristics of serfdom and feudalism. It could not be developed out of a system of middle-sized tenant farms, such as exists in Great Britain, or out of a developed and civilised peasant proprietorship like that of France, or again out of the homestead farming characteristic of the United States and Canada. In industry, the Russians were able to build on the models of large-scale, and largely of American, Capitalism, because what industry existed in Czarist Russia was largely of an imported type, directly imitative of the more advanced capitalist countries. But Russian agriculture was essentially primitive, and retained many of the collective qualities of medieval peasant economy. The Communists have sought to use this primitive collectivism as a foundation for their peasant Collectives, without passing the agricultural system through the intervening phase of a developed individualist farming economy.

Again, class-divisions in Russia were far clearer cut, at any rate in the towns, than they are in Western countries. In the villages the *kulaks*, or richer peasants, who usually employed some labour and were often dealers in other men's produce as well as their own, did form a large intermediate class, corresponding in some measure to the extensive *petite bourgeoisie* of the more advanced countries. But the urban middle class was relatively small, and far more largely dependent on minor public office: so that the fall of the old administrative system destroyed its influence. The technicians in the factories included a high proportion of foreigners, most of whom disappeared during the revolutionary struggle. The proletariat, small in numbers in relation to the peasantry, was a far more homogeneous and uniformly exploited class than are the manual workers in the Western countries; and the large average size of Russian factories gave this class a cohesion which is lacking in countries of more diversified industrial structure. The shortage of technicians made the technical problem of re-establishing productive efficiency very difficult indeed; but it had the compensation that it left a far smaller intermediate class to blur the significance of the revolutionary struggle and, by throwing the exploited proletariat more exclusively upon its own resources, provoked a mass-response which has been invaluable to the engineers of the new economic system. The Communists could not have been nearly so ruthless in 'liquidating' the *kulaks* in the villages if there had been in the towns a large intermediate class of *petits bourgeois* to join forces with them in resisting proletarianisation.

It may be argued that this would have been all to the good; for the ruthless 'liquidation' of the *kulaks* is not only by far the ugliest chapter of the record of revolutionary Russia, but also the part of Communist policy which, since the institution of the first Five-Year Plan, has brought the Soviet Government nearest to collapse. Enforced collectivisation, accompanied by the stamping out of the *kulaks*, was responsible for removing from Russian agriculture a large proportion of the less inefficient cultivators, and also for the devastating slaughter of live stock which occurred during the drive of 1930–1932. Nothing save a recognition that Russia is still in many respects a barbarous country can extenuate the inhuman severity of this drive against the *kulaks;* but the 'realists' of the Communist Party will argue that without this ferocity of repression it would have been impossible to get up the steam that was needed to make the new system work, and that the extermination of the *kulaks* as a class was an indispensable step towards collectivising the minds as well as the agrarian practice of the Russian peasantry.

I do not accept this contention. The ruthless suppression of the *kulaks* does seem to me both morally indefensible and also economically wrong in that it involved a slaughter of live stock which it must take many years to rectify and in this and other ways helped to precipitate the famine of 1933. But my purpose here is not to praise or condemn Stalin's agrarian policy, but to point out how essentially different the land problem would be in any country in which the *kulaks* were not, as in Russia, a small fraction of the entire peasantry but rather the predominant group—or at any rate where the main body of cultivators consisted of homestead farmers or peasant owners with a 'stake in the country.' Whatever might be the appropriate policy under these conditions, assuredly it could not include either the wholesale liquidation of the *kulaks* on the Russian model or the institution of farming methods at all resembling those of the *kolkhoz*, or collective farm.

There is yet another vital difference between the problem which confronted the Russians when they set on foot their first Five-Year Plan and that which would face any Government determined to institute a planned economy in an advanced Western country. The Communist leaders in 1928 had not only to plan the output of industry, but actually to create the industrial structure by means of which the planned output was to be achieved. They set out not merely to use and develop gradually an existing industrial machine, but to turn their country in a few years into an advanced industrial State. There were many reasons why this seemed to them indispensable. An advanced industrial structure was needed to make Russia safe for Communism in face of a hostile capitalist world; for a developed industrialism is the necessary foundation in these days of any effective military power. Moreover, Communism stood for a general raising of the standard of life; and this was clearly out of the question without the intensive development of those methods of mass-production which had made possible the far higher standards actually achieved in the great capitalist countries. Finally, the Communists believed in the historic civilising mission of the proletariat, and in the proletariat as the child of the technical revolution in industry. They wanted to swell the numbers and heighten the consciousness of the proletariat in Russia; and how could this be achieved except by industrialisation on the grand scale? All these considerations went together to cause the Communist leaders to press on as rapidly as they could with their projects of large-scale industrial development.

But the immediate cost of pursuing this policy was bound to be high. Since Great Britain took the lead in the development of capitalist industrialism in the course of the eighteenth century, no country has been industrialised without the help of considerable amounts of borrowed foreign capital; and even Great Britain was not transformed into a great capitalist power without using the profits of an extensive foreign commerce and the spoils of Empire as sources of investible capital to supplement the resources made available by domestic 'abstinence.'

Ordinarily, when industrialism develops in a 'new' country, the initial pace of growth is fairly slow, and the import of capital from abroad makes it unnecessary for the standard of living to be reduced in order to release labour for the production of capital goods. As the pace gets more rapid, foreign investment also increases, and the additional output secured by the earlier doses of industrialisation is available to offset the diversion of resources from the production of consumers' goods for domestic use. Thus the transition is made without a fall in the standard of living, and often to the accompaniment of a positive advance. This is easiest where a sparse population is in possession of large natural resources which are coming to offer highly profitable opportunities for exploitation, because there is an expanding demand for the new products in the world market.

In the absence of these conditions, or at least some of them, industrialisation is possible only at the cost of present abstinence. This is most of all the case where the country has a large population existing at a low standard of life; for in such cases the resources needed for capital development can ill be spared from current consumption. Moreover, until a country is already industrialised to a considerable extent it cannot easily produce for itself the instruments required for its industrialisation, however abstinent its citizens are prepared to be. It must, unless the pace of growth is to be extraordinarily slow and its method extraordinarily uneconomic, at least begin by acquiring from more advanced countries, which possess the technique of making such things, a considerable quantity of the more complicated instruments of production which it is setting out to install. Even if it proposes to make its own machinery, it must begin by importing foreign machine-making machinery in order to get a start. Where the necessary imports cannot be acquired on loan, by the investment of foreign capital, they will have to be paid for by exports of such goods as the country has to offer. These will be, in such a case, mainly raw materials and foodstuffs; and it will be possible to speed up the pace of industrialisation only by either exporting foodstuffs which are badly wanted at home, or diverting labour from producing foodstuffs to producing raw materials for export, or of course by combining both methods.

Now if, while this is being done, anything happens seriously to depress the prices which these exports of foodstuffs and materials can command in the world market, in relation to the prices of the industrial goods for which they are needed to pay, either industrialisation will have to be slowed down, or domestic abstinence will have to be pushed to more extreme lengths in order to make up the requisite quantity of foreign exchange. In other words, either the hope of increasing output in the future will have to be scaled down, or there will have to be a further fall in the current standard of living.

These are, of course, precisely the difficulties which have confronted the U.S.S.R. since 1929.

SOCIALIST PLANNING—THE U.S.S.R.

The relative prices of agricultural products had been sagging for some time before the world depression set in; but hardly had the first Five-Year Plan begun when there was simultaneously a sharp fall in the exchange value of the goods which the Soviet Union had to sell and a shrinkage in the demand, intensified by the growth of tariffs, quotas and other barriers in the way of international trade. But the Communists dared not draw back from the ambitious schemes of industrialisation which they had just begun to carry into effect. They had, therefore, to force exports on to the unwelcoming world market at the cost of the immediate standard of living at home; and they had also to produce at home many complicated capital goods which they would in more favourable circumstances undoubtedly have purchased abroad. The 'tempo' proposed for the Five-Year Plan was ambitious when it was first projected: it became more than ambitious when the world depression had put formidable fresh obstacles in its way.

It was possible in these circumstances to go forward or back, but not to stand still. The plan could have been abandoned or slowed down, and the N.E.P. restored, at least in part, in the hope of stimulating higher agricultural production. This would have involved diverting industrial resources from the making of capital goods for further industrialisation to the supplying of goods which could be given to the peasants in exchange for their food. It would have meant a higher immediate standard of life, but at the cost of lessening the military strength of the Soviet Union and postponing the development of a modern industrial technique. Stalin and his associates firmly rejected that alternative, and chose instead to press on at full speed with the original plan. But under the changed conditions this involved much more severe abstinence for workers and peasants alike. The Soviet authorities would inevitably have less industrial goods to offer the peasants in exchange for food than they had hoped and expected when the plan was worked out. Under these conditions, Stalin decided to alter almost at a blow the entire basis of Russia's agricultural economy. Left to produce individually, the peasants were certain to meet a fall in the supply of industrial goods by slowing down the production of agricultural commodities. Very well, that meant that individual peasant agriculture would have to go at once instead of later, and be replaced by a collective system which would be more amenable to the control of the planning authorities.

It was hoped by this drive for collectivisation to increase agricultural output, and secure more foodstuffs both for provisioning the towns and for export. Actually, the immediate consequences on agricultural output were exceedingly adverse, above all because of the immense slaughter of livestock by *kulaks* and other peasants who either lacked the means of feeding them or were unwilling to hand them over to the new collective farms. A bad harvest over a large part of the U.S.S.R. made the situation still worse. There was in certain areas a terrible famine, which almost wrecked the entire development of the plan. But Stalin held on grimly, though he did for a time suspend further measures of collectivisation; and at last the worst was over, and after many deaths the Russian peasants settled down to work under the new system of collective, or co-operative, farming.

It is not surprising that these accumulated difficulties of the Soviet Union led to a severe intensification of the dictatorship. The *kulaks*, who might have rallied the peasants against collectivisation, were ruthlessly 'liquidated,' though they included many of the most competent farmers. In town as well as country, the G.P.U. became more active. There was more heresy-hunting, in order both to find shoulders to bear the blame of the current distress and to tighten up discipline in the Communist Party and the factories and so secure the last ounce of concentrated effort behind the execution of the plan. Furthermore, when all had to go short, the award of less inadequate rations became an immensely powerful stimulus to effort. Shock-workers, and all who distinguished themselves by zeal and energy in making the plan succeed, were rewarded with higher pay and preferential treatment. The plan was not fully executed in most branches of industry; but in view of the mountainous difficulties to be overcome, what was achieved was nothing short of marvellous. The price of success, however, was one which assuredly no Western proletariat, less enduring than the Russian, less accustomed to being exploited to the very limit, and used to a far higher standard of living, could ever be induced to pay.

Fortunately, as we have seen, there ought to be no need, in any Western country, to ask for such a sacrifice. All the Western countries have already an industrial equipment capable, in almost all branches, of producing a good deal more than is being currently produced. They have no shortage of skilled labour, and the construction of the new plant required even for a very ambitious plan of economic development would make relatively small calls upon their peoples for abstinence from current consumption. Their first problem, in introducing a planned economy, is less the creation of new productive resources than the fuller use of resources which they already possess.

These differences make Russian planning in many respects unfruitful of lessons by which the Western countries can profit. Nevertheless, there are certain features of Russian planning which are independent of the peculiar and highly unfavourable conditions under which it had to be introduced —certain problems common to all economies planned on a Socialist basis, and certain solutions of these problems to which it is well worth while to direct our attention. In the first place any planned economic system involves the existence of an authority, or of authorities, invested with the power of deciding, at least broadly, what is to be produced. Such a decision involves, in the first place, a planned allocation of the available resources between 'investment' and current consumption, and secondly within these two broad categories of production a further allocation between different industries and kinds of output. In Russia, in the first Five-Year Plan, the main emphasis was put, for reasons given already, on the production of capital goods and of those durable consumers' goods which had to be provided in conjunction with them—such as housing accommodation in the new and growing centres of industrial development. The consumer, as such, had to play second fiddle for the time. His reward was postponed to the day when the new capital goods would at length begin to pour out an increasing stream of commodities for his use.

The Russian Plans therefore allocated an exceedingly high proportion of the available resources to the production of investment goods. In the four and a half years of the first Five-Year Plan there was achieved a total investment of 60,000,000,000 roubles, of which 46,000,000,000 went into industrial development. Between 1928 and 1932 the share of means of production in the total output of large-scale industry rose from 44 per cent to 72 per cent.

The same authorities were responsible for allocating resources between investment and consumption and for deciding broadly what goods were to be produced within these two great sections of the entire economy. The Gosplan, or State Planning Commission, proposed what should be produced, partly on its own initiative and partly on the basis of plans sent up to it by the Commissariats for Heavy and Light Industry, for Transport, for Agriculture, and for the various social services, as well as by 'trusts' and other authorities in particular industries and by planning bodies in the various geographical divisions of the U.S.S.R. But Gosplan had no final or executive authority. Its plans needed endorsement or amendment by the Council of People's Commissaries and its economic organ, the Council of Labour and Defence; and they had to be executed by the various Commissariats of the Soviet Union as a whole and of its constituent Republics and lesser territorial divisions. Gosplan was a planning body, and was neither a deciding nor an executive authority.

On what basis were these vital decisions recommended, made, and subsequently implemented by

SOCIALIST PLANNING—THE U.S.S.R.

the various bodies entrusted with their execution? In a planless economy no similar decisions have to be made at all. The State, even in such an economy, does indeed decide how much to spend on those economic services for which it makes itself directly responsible, and does largely govern, wherever it gives grants in aid, the orders placed by local government agencies for schools, houses and other capital goods provided under public auspices. But for the rest the course of production is left to the separate decisions of a host of *entrepreneurs*, ranging in size from huge trusts and combines to 'independent workers' employing no one except themselves; and these decisions are guided by the motive of maximum profit in the light of the current structure of money costs on the one hand and the various types of demand on the other. The essential thing about these decisions is that they are unrelated. They cannot, for obvious reasons, add up to more than the total of the available resources of production—the pricing system will see to that. But they can, and often do, add up to less. Nor is there any necessary relationship between the quantities of various goods that *entrepreneurs* decide to produce, and the quantities consumers want—though, to the extent to which the *entrepreneurs* act wisely, from the profitmaking standpoint, production will tend to be adjusted to consumers' demand, up to the limit at which it becomes more profitable to withhold goods from the consumers.

In contradistinction, the planners in a Socialist economy set out from the assumption that the available productive resources are to be fully employed, and that consequently a decision to produce any one thing is necessarily a decision not to produce something else. The planners are considering, not what volume of production in a particular line of business will produce the maximum profit, but whether it will be most expedient to produce this thing or that thing, or more of one thing at the expense of producing less of another. Their decisions have to be taken in terms, not of anticipated money surpluses, but of real things. They are called upon to prefer this thing to that thing, using their judgment to decide which will better serve the ends which they have in view. Out of limited means of production how to achieve the best total result—that, and nothing else, is the problem which the controlling authorities of a planned economy have to face.

But how, say the orthodox economists, are they to decide, save by submitting themselves to the test of consumers' desires, and trying to produce what by the evidence of demand-prices the consumers appear to want? There are two reasons why, in a planned economy, this test of the consumers' desires is bound to break down. I do not refer to the fact that, in any economy, the State and its subordinate organs, by commanding directly the production of certain things, such as schools, roads and public buildings, do in fact substitute the criterion of public need for the individual choice of private consumers, who might, if let alone, demand either more or less of such things than the State elects to supply. That divergence between consumers' private valuations and the actual supply of goods and services exists in any economy, planned or unplanned; and the most a planned economy can do in that field is to widen the range of collective supply. I have in mind two other respects in which the criteria of a planned economy are bound to differ from those of an individualist system of enterprise.

In the first place, the structure of consumers' demand depends on the prices at which the various goods are offered for sale. In determining prices, the planning authority will be, to a considerable extent, fixing the level of demand for each type of goods. And, if it is answered that pricing in a planned economy will be according to cost of production, that only raises a second point; for cost of production will evidently depend on the quantity of each thing it is decided to produce, on the prices charged for the factors of production—that is, ultimately, for the types of labour employed—and on the allocations of capital made for the development of the industry in question—for the extent of capital development is obviously a factor of the first importance in determining cost.

A planless economy, in which each *entrepreneur* takes his decisions apart from the rest, obviously confronts each *entrepreneur* with a broadly given structure of costs, represented by the current levels of wages, rent and interest. But in a planned Socialist economy this is not the case; for these charges may not exist at all, or, if they do exist, they do so not as objective factors beyond the control of the collective *entrepreneur*, but as charges determined by that *entrepreneur* as elements in the economic plan. How far wages continue to exist depends on the methods adopted by the planned economy in distributing incomes to the citizens: how far rent exists depends on the decision of the collective *entrepeneur* to make at a level which it decides, or not to make at all, a charge for the use of land and other rentable property by its constituent enterprises: whether interest exists depends on the decision of the collective *entrepreneur* to make or not to make a money charge for the use of capital and credit. All these charges can be made, or not made; and, if they are made, the rates at which they are made are bound to be controlled rates, determined by the collective *entrepreneur* in one capacity and paid by this same *entrepreneur* in another capacity. Such charges may possibly serve a valuable purpose in cost-accounting; but they are utterly different in nature from the objective costs which the *entrepreneurs* in a planless capitalist economy have to meet.

Accordingly, in a planned Socialist economy there can be no objective structure of money costs. Costs can be *imputed*, to any desired extent; and indeed, as long as any money costs at all remain in being they must be imputed, to that extent at least. But these imputed costs are not objective, but *fiat* costs determined by the public policy of the State. The State decides, through its appropriate organs, what the levels of wages are to be for the various occupations, what rents are to be charged, what interest is to be paid on capital, what industry is to contribute by way of taxation to the expenses of the State—or it decides to abolish such charges altogether. To the extent to which it retains any of them, it is imputing costs at levels which it decides for itself.

But imputation can, if the State so desires, go much further than this; for costs can be imputed without being actually charged at all. Imputed wages, rent and interest costs can be chalked up against each separate enterprise belonging to the planned economy, without any money actually changing hands. This can be done on the ground that the imputation of these charges, though they are not to be actually paid, will provide valuable tests of the comparative efficiency of different enterprises and of the same enterprises at different times, and will enable a far better check to be kept on extravagance and slackness than could possibly be kept without the use of such methods of cost-accounting.

To a certain extent this is undeniably true, at any rate in the transition stages to a completely developed system of economic planning. But the expediency of such methods does not alter the fact that the structure of imputed costs is bound to be arbitrary. It is perfectly possible to impute an interest charge for all capital or credit used in each enterprise within a Socialist economy; but the rate at which the charge is made can be only an arbitrary rate determined by the collective authority itself. Similarly with rent, or wages, or any other costs—they can be charged, or chalked up without being charged; but the rates at which they are charged are bound to be *fiat* rates.

It is, however, quite a mistake to suppose that this fact destroys their usefulness. For the planned economy will not be using them as means of deciding upon the distribution of the available productive resources, but only as means of checking the efficiency of Socialist enterprise. For the purpose of determining how much capital and credit an enterprise is using up, the rate of interest is quite irrelevant. So is the rate of wages for determining the amount of labour, or that of rents for determining the amount of land. The allocation of resources in a Socialist economy will be made in terms of the real things available, and not of the money values that may be imputed to them. The purpose of imputation, if it exists, is not to settle the allocation, but to check the efficiency of the use.

But, the orthodox economist will object, unless all the factors of production can be expressed in commensurable terms—and how can they, save in terms of money values?—there will be no means of settling with economic rightness either between alternative methods of production, or between alternative kinds of product. A given commodity can be produced, say, either with more capital and less labour, or with less capital and more labour. How, save in terms of money cost, is a choice between these alternative methods to be made? The answer is that it can be made, without involving the money standard at all, by comparing the real quantities of labour, including labour employed in capital construction, that each alternative will use up. But this, it will be objected, involves the commensurability of different kinds of labour, even if it avoids the measurement of labour against money capital. So it does; but not in the sense that requires the measurement of the marginal money productivities of the different kinds of labour involved. For a planned economy, the actual plenty or scarcity of different kinds of labour is a far more relevant consideration in deciding which method of production ought to be employed than the relative wage-costs of the alternatives. Doubtless, the planned wage-rates may be so fixed as to expand the supply of one kind of labour, and to contract that of another, if wages are retained as a method of distributing incomes. But the relative supplies of different kinds of skill will in fact depend far more on the vocational training provided by the planned economy than on any other factor.

The decision between alternative methods of production in a planned economy will in fact be made in the light of a number of considerations, among which relative money cost will play only a quite minor part, if it plays any part at all, and is not rather a consequence than a cause of planned decisions about the allocation of real resources. Plenty and scarcity of different kinds of skill, irksomeness or pleasantness of one occupation as against another, the degree of willingness to postpone present for the sake of future consumption—factors of these kinds will primarily influence the planned economy in reaching its decisions. In many cases there will be no doubt at all about the superiority of a new method of production over one already in use; and in such cases the only question will be the rate at which the supersession of the old method by the new one is to be effected. In other cases there will be real doubt; but the relative money costs of the two processes, even if they could be ascertained, would not be the decisive factor in determining the choice between them. The basis of choice will be judgment, involving a weighing up of numerous considerations, some of which do not admit of quantitative expression. The planning authority will do what seems best in the light of all the circumstances, using money cost only as one aid to judgment, and not as the decisive thing.

Similarly, the decision between alternative final products will be made in the light of needs, rather than money costs. Real costs, in the sense of the amounts of scarce factors used up in the processes of production, are of course highly relevant. But it is not necessary that all the real costs should be capable of expression in quantitatively commensurable terms. Perhaps it would be nicer if they could all be expressed in these terms; but they simply cannot, in any economy, however planned or however planless it may be. For it is a travesty of the truth to identify the money costs, which are commensurable in a capitalist economy, with real costs. In the light of these money costs the *entrepreneurs* in a planless economy do make decisions; but there is no assurance at all that these decisions, even when they are 'right' from a profit-making point of view, serve to secure a preference for the smallest real cost with which the ends of production can be achieved. The measurement of money costs is the measurement of money costs, and nothing more, within the structure of such costs which is determined by the nature and conditions of the particular economy in which they exist. It cannot express real costs; for real costs are, to a very great extent, incommensurable in quantitative terms. The 'real cost' of the same man's labour for two hours may be assumed to be twice the real cost of his labour for one hour, provided that his total labour has not been so prolonged as to raise the real cost of the last hour. But there is no strictly quantitative way of measuring absolutely the real cost of one man's labour against another's, much less of making the real cost of all the diverse and intricate processes of production absolutely commensurable.

Imputed costs are always relative, never absolute. They are relative to the value standards of the economy within which they exist; and they change with every change in these standards. In capitalist societies money costs are objective from the standpoint of the individual *entrepreneur*, and thus appear to afford an objective standard for the society as a whole. But they are in reality no more than the money expression of the particular standards by which the society measures such real costs as it is equipped, or minded, to measure at all.

In a collective economy, where there exists but a single *entrepreneur*, however subdivided for reasons of convenience in administration, there can be no

SOCIALIST PLANNING—THE U.S.S.R.

appearance of an objective standard. For the values put upon things are put upon them by the *entrepreneur*, at any rate as far as factors of production are concerned. In the case of finished goods offered for sale to the members of the community, there is more appearance of an objective standard; for the consumers will prefer one thing to another, and shift their preferences according to the relative prices of different goods. But these consumers' preferences reflect the income structure of the society, which is under collective control: so that here too the apparently objective standard embodies large elements which are the deliberate creations of the collective authority. Consumers' preferences remain real; but they appear only as reactions to offers by the collective *entrepreneur* of certain goods at certain prices; and even so the general character of these reactions is determined by the policy of the economy as a whole.

In these circumstances, the test of the worthwhileness of producing any particular thing cannot be simply the relation of the price-offer which it elicits to its money cost of production. This is one test, no doubt, but only one, and by no means the final test. The primary function of the collective planning authority is to allocate resources to production in the light of estimates of needs, and therewith to plan the allocation of incomes in such a way as to give the best prospect that the more pressing needs will receive satisfaction. This does not mean that the planning authority is to force unwanted goods upon the consumers, but only that it will do its planning in terms of real things and not of money. In making its allocations of resources it will be guided by what the consumers are most likely to want to buy with the means at their disposal, and it will be prepared constantly to alter its allocations in the light of the evidence afforded by the actual state of consumers' demand. But it will not take consumers' demand as an objective standard, because it will be well aware that it can at any time be altered by altering the distribution of incomes in the community.

In the U.S.S.R. the acute shortage of almost every kind of goods has in one sense simplified the planning problem; for there is usually little doubt concerning men's basic needs, however much there may be about their requirements when their basic needs have been met. Under the first Five-Year Plan two problems took pride of place. The first, as we have seen, was that of deciding to what extent the current wants of the consumers were to be postponed to the claims of capital accumulation, with the object of improving the national strength and making a larger output of consumers' goods possible later on. Having pitched their claims on behalf of accumulation exceedingly high, the Soviet planners were left with only a very limited power to produce goods for current consumption. Agricultural production, being still for the most part in the hands of peasant cultivators, could be only indirectly controlled under the plan; and, in order to persuade the peasants to produce more, it was necessary to provide an increased supply of industrial goods for sale to them in exchange. This second need had to be harmonised with the need to meet as far as possible the demands of the urban population for industrial goods.

Accordingly, the Soviet planners were compelled to think for the most part directly in terms of real goods and real factors of production that would be used up in making them; and the problem of 'cost' occupied in the earlier stages a quite minor position. There was no doubt of everything that could be produced being eagerly snapped up, if it was offered at a price that consumers could possibly afford. Provided that the prices and the incomes available for use in buying goods balanced, there could be no question of unwanted goods remaining unsold; for consumers' needs were too clamant for any hoarding to occur. In these circumstances there was no need for any elaborate measures to gauge demand. Consumers could be relied upon to snap up what was offered, and ask for more up to the very limit of their incomes, without too nice a scrutiny of one thing offered as against another. The urban consumers, who badly needed more food, could get it only by going short of industrial products; and the peasant saw his best hope of getting more industrial products in growing more food for the market.

Even after the collectivisation of the greater part of Russian agriculture, the nature of the problem was not greatly changed. Under the second Five-Year Plan the claims of capital accumulation have been somewhat relaxed, though they still remain very high. Provision is made for a larger, and growing, supply of consumers' goods; but it is still true that the elementary needs of the population are too far off being satisfied for much doubt to arise about the directions in which production should be expanded, or for consumers to develop finikin preferences that it is difficult to foresee. The difficult problems of choosing between expanding the supply of this as against that sort of consumers' goods have not yet arisen in Russia. They cannot arise in a serious form until a much fuller satisfaction of primary wants has been secured.

Of course, this does not exempt the planners from the possibility of making an unwise allocation of the available resources between different types of production. It is quite possible that the inhabitants of the U.S.S.R. would prefer, if they had a free choice, a slower rate of capital accumulation, and also that they would get more satisfaction out of a different distribution of the resources applied to the making of consumers' goods. Planners are certainly

SOCIALIST PLANNING—THE U.S.S.R.   77

not exempt from making mistakes, apart from the fact that they may have standards of desirability which diverge from those of the individual consumers, even under a planned system of distributing incomes. But when there is a clamant need for almost everything, the broad desirable allocation of such resources as are available for meeting the consumers' needs is not very difficult to arrive at, and mistakes, as distinct from divergences of deliberate policy, in allocating resources are not likely to be very serious.

The Russians, in their Five-Year Plans, have planned to produce so many pairs of boots, so many suits of clothes, so many household utensils of various sorts, so many of a variety of consumable commodities; and in this allocation of resources to various uses the question of money cost has hardly arisen at all. The problem has been that of finding the labour and the machinery needed for producing these things. Nevertheless the Soviet planners have from the first attempted to give their decisions a monetary as well as a real expression—to plan money costs as well as real outputs. But the purpose of this costing has been not to determine how much of each thing it is desirable to produce, but rather to keep a check on the efficiency with which the production already decided upon is being carried into effect. At least, this was undoubtedly true in the earlier stages of the plan.

Latterly, however, costs, reckoned in terms of

money, have come to occupy a more important place. There has been a growing insistence that, save for special reasons clearly shown, each accounting unit in the Soviet economy—individual factories, 'trusts' covering a group of factories, 'combinations' or 'syndicates' combining a whole industry—shall show balanced production budgets. This is often regarded as meaning that the Soviet economy is returning to the capitalist principle of determining the worthwhileness of production by balancing selling prices against costs. But it need not mean this, and I doubt if in fact it does. For it must not be forgotten that the prices at which Soviet institutions sell their goods are controlled prices, which are commonly fixed in relation to estimated levels of cost. The question, then, is not fundamentally whether the individual Soviet enterprise 'pays' but whether its actual costs are being kept down to the level of its estimated costs. The requirement of balanced factory budgets is really a requirement of an adequate standard of efficiency in the actual execution of a planned programme of production, and not an attempt to reimpose the capitalist criterion of profit. A Soviet factory that is compelled to close down, and is reopened under new management, suffers this fate not because it is unprofitable, but because it is convicted of inefficiency.

I do not say that the criterion of 'profitableness' is never applied, but only that it occupies a quite

SOCIALIST PLANNING—THE U.S.S.R. 79

subordinate place. To the extent to which 'luxuries' are produced at all, the profit criterion does reappear; for it is regarded as fair that those who consume luxuries should pay dearly for them, and accordingly they will not be produced except under conditions which will yield high profits. But this does not mean that luxuries are produced in preference to necessaries wherever their production would be more profitable. It means only that, when some concession is made to the demand for luxuries, profit is exacted as a by-product, much as some capitalist States impose high taxes on wines and spirits and other forms of luxury consumption.

Moreover, the Soviet planners are doubtless guided by considerations of cost over a far wider field when they are considering what lines of production offer the best prospects of increasing return with an expanded output. They will energetically push the production of those goods which seem to offer the most favourable opportunities for mass-production. But here the matter is one of real, rather than of money costs, the aim being rather to release productive resources for other uses than to obtain a surplus over costs by the sale of the goods. Indeed, it seems probable that the goods which offer the best prospects of increasing return will be sold at marginal prices in order to encourage their consumption, and that higher prices in relation to costs are more likely to be attached to goods of which the consumption is to be discouraged: so that the larger surpluses may in fact be realised by the sale of those products which the Soviet planners are least eager to push.

On the whole, in the Soviet economy selling prices are based on costs of production, and are coming to be so to an increasing extent. But the costs on which prices are based are controlled costs, dependent on the levels of remuneration fixed for workers of different kinds, on the charges made for the use of capital and credit, and on the taxes levied on the various enterprises. Of these controlled costs, the cost of labour is obviously by far the most important; and it is therefore necessary to endeavour to understand on what basis the Soviet economy sets out to fix wages and salaries.

The problem of remuneration in the transition between Capitalism and Socialism was discussed long ago by Marx in his *Critique on the Gotha Programme*. Marx there proclaimed the principle 'From each according to his capacities, to each according to his needs' as the only rule of distribution for a fully developed Communist society. But he held this principle to be inapplicable in the transition stage, for which he proclaimed instead the principle of unequal remuneration according to the value of the work done by the individual. Under Capitalism, Marx argued, the worker has a part of the value of his product filched from him by the capitalist—surplus value. A Socialist society, even in the stage of transition, will have abolished surplus value; and the whole product will be at its disposal. Out of the gross product it will have first to set aside what is needed both to meet the depreciation of capital and to create an insurance fund against mishaps, and to make provision for the accumulation of additional capital on whatever scale may be thought to be desirable. There remains, Marx says, the part of the product that is destined for current consumption. Out of this must be met the general expenses of administration and of the social services which it is decided to supply collectively, as well as the maintenance of all those who are unable to work. Only what is left remains to be distributed to the workers as wages or salaries. After all these deductions, Marx holds, the individual worker in the transitional stage to full Communism will receive back in proportion to what he gives to society—the equivalent of his individual quantum of labour.

The Soviet leaders are endeavouring faithfully to follow out this doctrine of Marx, and to make the rewards of the producers commensurate with their individual labour services. But how is the magnitude of these services to be determined? It cannot be purely by the number of hours worked; for according to Marxian principles skilled labour counts as a multiple of common labour, and the worker who produces more than his fellows in the course of an hour is producing more than an hour's worth of socially necessary labour. Within a single occupation, the relative claims can be assessed in accordance with variations in output, wherever output is individually measurable. But this will not avail to determine the appropriate relative levels for different sorts of labour. To the extent to which the more skilled types of labour are producible at will by special training, it can be answered that their relative remunerations should depend on the costs of training skilled workers of different kinds. But this cannot apply to types of ability that are not producible at will by training or selection, any more than the 'value' of naturally scarce commodities can depend on the labour involved in producing them. Moreover, if the cost of training is met by the community, it is not clear why the benefit should accrue to the individual in whom the community has made an investment.

Marx, in his *Critique on the Gotha Programme*, does not discuss these difficulties, contenting himself with the statement that remuneration in accordance with work done will be the rule of a transitional economy. He fully recognises that this rule has no final validity, and is in effect no more than a survival from the era of Capitalism, altered by the discontinuance of the capitalist appropriation of surplus value. It would probably

SOCIALIST PLANNING—THE U.S.S.R.   83

not have disturbed him to be told that the net value of each individual's labour is in fact unascertainable, and that all a transitional economy could in fact do would be to take over from Capitalism the current *relative* valuations of labour-power of different kinds, supplement the wages paid under Capitalism with such part of the socialised surplus value as was not absorbed by the necessary deductions mentioned above, and thereafter modify relative valuations in particular cases in accordance with considerations of expediency, so as to equate supply and demand of the various kinds of labour, and make such reductions in the inequality of remuneration between different occupations as the changed economic and social structure rendered possible.

This is, in fact, what the Soviet authorities have done. They have taken over the pre-revolutionary wage-standards, scaled down the remuneration of the higher salaried workers, scaled up the remuneration of the lower grades, modified wage-scales so as to attract labour into occupations in which there has been a shortage, and aimed at increasing wage-standards in general as fast as resources could be spared from providing for intensive accumulation of capital. They have created an economy in which, thanks to the abolition of surplus value and the destruction of class monopolies of entry into certain occupations, the range of difference in income is far narrower than in capitalist societies. But they have also admitted and even encouraged inequality to any extent to which they have regarded it as requisite for securing the right kinds of labour, or eliciting the best obtainable effort in the service of productive efficiency. Treating these methods of remuneration as merely transitional to a system of distribution based upon needs—to a purely Communist system —they are not perturbed if there can be found for them no logical basis. Are they not a hang-over from the illogicalities and contradictions of the capitalist system; and is it not therefore natural that they should be illogical and self-contradictory?

Wages, determined in this fashion, provide for the Soviet economy a basis of money costs, upon which the pricing of goods is partly founded. But the prices so determined can be raised or lowered to any extent wherever this seems expedient, without the changed relation between costs and selling prices having any necessary effect on the volume of goods which it is decided to produce. The change in prices will be, in fact, the consequence and not the cause of a decision to produce more or less; and it will have no necessary reaction on the wages to be paid to the producers. For, according to the Marxian view, the wages in the transition should depend on the 'value' of the product—that is, on the amount of socially necessary labour involved in producing it—and not upon the price, which bears no fixed proportion to the 'value.'

SOCIALIST PLANNING—THE U.S.S.R.   85

The Soviet economy has, then, a cost structure and a price structure. But the relationship between these two structures is radically different from that which exists in capitalist societies. The course of production is not determined, save to a quite minor extent, by this relationship. The price structure is to some extent designed, as it must be in any economy which uses the method of offering goods for sale, to ration the goods in accordance with consumers' ability and willingness to pay for them, or in other words to cut off demand at the point at which no further supply is available. But hitherto this has not been at all generally the case; for of many things more would have been bought at the prevailing price if there had been a larger supply. Prices, however, were not raised so as to equalise supply and demand. Instead, the method of rationing was used in some cases, and in others preference was given in getting supplies to certain types of distributive agency over others, in order that the limited supplies might come into what were regarded as the right hands. It was, however, from the first clearly the intention to let these forms of rationing lapse as fast as supplies could be made more adequate, and to let prices for most goods come to the levels which will balance demand with supply. Rationing has, in fact, already almost disappeared.

As for costs, their function in the Soviet economy is far less that of governing the volume of output of this or that commodity by their relationship to selling prices than that of providing a test of efficiency by enabling actual to be measured against anticipated costs. Considerations of cost do enter in when output is being planned, but only side by side with other considerations, which may be allowed to prevail against them. For the aim of Soviet economy is not, like that of capitalist economy, to realise maximum profit, but rather to achieve maximum satisfaction of collectively estimated needs and desires. The intensity of consumers' demand, as measured by price-offers, is one factor of which account is taken in deciding between alternative forms of production. But it is only one factor; and it does not necessarily carry the day.

In other words, Soviet planning is based primarily on considerations of collectively estimated social need. This criterion is relatively easy to apply to most forms of output in a society as poor as Soviet Russia still is, the chief difficulty at this stage being to strike the best balance between current consumption and capital accumulation. It is, however, bound to offer increasing difficulty as the standard of living rises; for, when the elementary needs have been generally satisfied, productive activity must be increasingly occupied with goods and services of which the consumption is a matter of individual choice and preference, and not of general need. As this stage is reached, intelligent planning calls increasingly for a correct anticipation of the consumers' desires, which can be expressed most easily in their willingness to pay for one thing rather than another. In this field, in which there is no reason for the State to encourage one kind of consumption against another for social reasons, the obviously correct course is to base prices on costs of production or, where one product offers superior opportunities for a lowering of cost through larger output, to lower its price in order to extend the market for it at the expense of demand for commodities which have to be produced at constant or increasing cost.

A cost structure is therefore vital in all those fields of production which create, not general necessaries, but articles of optional consumption—a consumption which must include the consumption even of general necessaries in amounts beyond the minimum required for a tolerable basic standard of life. Such a cost structure, in a Socialist economy, can have no absolutely objective basis. It can only result from the decisions of the economy concerning the relative levels of remuneration for different types of work and the charges, if any, made or imputed for the use of other factors of production. These decisions, because they determine the cost structure, must influence the decisions of the planners about the quantities of various kinds of goods which are to be produced. In the transitional economy, in which labour costs continue to be measured in money paid out as wages and salaries, the course of production will tend to follow, for all goods above the level of general necessaries, the relation of these socially determined costs to consumers' preparedness to pay, which is in turn affected by the distribution of incomes. But as the economy approaches more nearly to complete Communism, replacing remuneration for work done by the allocation of incomes according to need, the costs of production melt away, or rather cease to be measurable in terms of the payments made to the individual producers of any particular commodity.

As this happens, money costs actually incurred can, if it seems desirable, be replaced by purely accounting costs imputed by continuing to value the different sorts of labour according to their social productivities. But it seems far more probable that, by the time this position has been reached for any substantial part of the social output, a new standard of non-monetary measurement will have been devised for estimating the relative worthwhileness of different branches of production. This standard will most likely be expressed in terms not of money but of units of real productive energy used up—in 'ergs,' to borrow a term popularised in America by the technocrats a year or two ago. Costs of producing various things will be measured against one another not in money, but in 'ergs'; and the test of worthwhileness will be found in the relationship between 'ergs' consumed and the intensity of the consumers' demands for the various products that it is possible to supply. Psychologists and physiologists, rather than economists, will provide the standards by which 'ergs' are to be measured for different occupations and types of labour; and consumers' money offers, for as long as such offers survive, will be compared with units of productive energy used up rather than with money costs of production.

This may appear to some readers a distinction rather than a difference. But it is really a vital difference. It is a source of confusion, and not enlightenment, to attempt to measure the real costs of production in the same units as are used for the measurement of the consumers' demands. The use of different accounting units for these two purposes will not make it harder to plan production so as to secure the largest net satisfaction of human needs and desires. On the contrary, it will facilitate the task, by making clear that productive energy is not a commodity to be bought and sold on the same terms as the commodities it can produce, but an independent category. The problem is to apply the available supply of units of productive energy to the best social purpose in satisfying the community's individual and collective needs and desires.

By thus balancing units of energy against units of consumers' demand, though they are not reduced to a common monetary form, the collective economy can achieve fully as workable a standard of measurement as it can by expressing both sides of the equation in terms of money, and can do this without the falsification involved in translating human energy into monetary terms, and on a basis wholly unaffected by the methods adopted for the distribution of incomes. The abolition of payment for work done does not involve the destruction of any quantitative standard for comparing costs and satisfactions. On the contrary, the new standard of measurement clarifies the whole problem by expressing essentially different things in different, yet comparable terms, instead of trying to reduce them to a common standard which is bound to be inappropriate to one or other.

The Soviet economy, still in the phase of transition between Capitalism and full Socialism, has not yet reached this stage; for it still retains the conception, which it has taken over from Capitalism, of remuneration for work done. But it is feeling its way towards the new standards; for while it continues to measure costs of production in money, it uses these measurements for the most part, not to determine what is to be produced, but rather as means of estimating the quantities of labour that are being used up in producing different things. It thus points the way towards an alternative standard, which it is not, and cannot yet be, in a position fully to apply.

CHAPTER III

FASCIST 'PLANNING'—GERMANY AND ITALY

THE Fascist countries—Italy and Germany—do not possess planned economies in anything like the same sense as the U.S.S.R. For it is a cardinal Fascist doctrine that private enterprise is to be preserved and fostered, and that the State is to supervise but not to administer industry. According to Fascist theories the capitalist employer, equally with the workmen and all other citizens, is a servant of the State, which lays upon him its commands in the interest of the whole nation. The employer's 'function' is to act, within his own business, as a leader and representative of the national economy, and he is accordingly invested with a special authority, conferred upon him by the State, in his dealings with his workmen. Their 'function,' as members of the national economy, is to carry out the employer's orders without question; and any indiscipline, such as strike action, on their part is immediately repressed. On the other hand, while the employer has full authority to issue orders which the workers are bound to obey, he has no right to declare a lock-out, which would interrupt productive activity and do the State harm.

If disputes arise between employers and workmen, the State itself will provide for their adjustment through special courts which it maintains for this purpose; and the decisions of these courts are binding on both parties. There is thus an appearance of equality between employer and workman before the law of the State; but even this formal equality exists only in respect of the prohibition of industrial disputes, and apart from this the superior status of the employer as leader of his section of the national economy is strongly asserted.

This description applies more fully to Germany than to Italy. For, whereas the Nazis have vehemently upheld the principle of personal leadership and authority in every sphere of public and economic life, the Italian Fascists, apart from the lonely eminence of *Il Duce*, have been more concerned to uphold, at any rate in theory, the principle of 'corporative' control. Germany is not and does not seek to be a Corporative State, but rather proclaims herself a State based on the universal assertion of personal leadership and authority. There is much in common between the absolutism of Hitler and the absolutism of Mussolini, but far less between the political and economic structures that have been built up under their several auspices. Germany represents the militarist principle of authoritarian discipline under personal leadership; Italy that of corporative organisation directed and controlled by the overriding authority of the Sovereign State.

Thus, in Italy, stress is laid on the principle of delegated corporative authority. Mussolini, *Il Duce*, is at the head of the State, with autocratic power; and, according to Fascist theory, Mussolini as head of the State possesses overriding authority over every person and institution in the State. But whereas in Germany we find under Hitler a host of lesser *Führers*, each in theory cock of his own particular dunghill, in Italy we find under Mussolini corporative institutions, each with its own appointed sphere of collective competence. Hitler asserts the dominance of the individual, Mussolini that of the functional group subordinated to a co-ordinating discipline by the State.

Yet it would be a great mistake to accept either of these pictures at its face value. In Italy the Corporations, supposed to be the principal functional organs of the Corporative State, were not brought into existence at all until 1934, and have as yet done hardly anything. Economic power remains, despite the Corporations, in the hands of the capitalist employers; and the State, directly or through the State-controlled banks, deals with the capitalist employers far more than with the Corporations when it is a question of deciding what economic policy is to be pursued. In Germany, on the other hand, the minor *Führers* appointed to

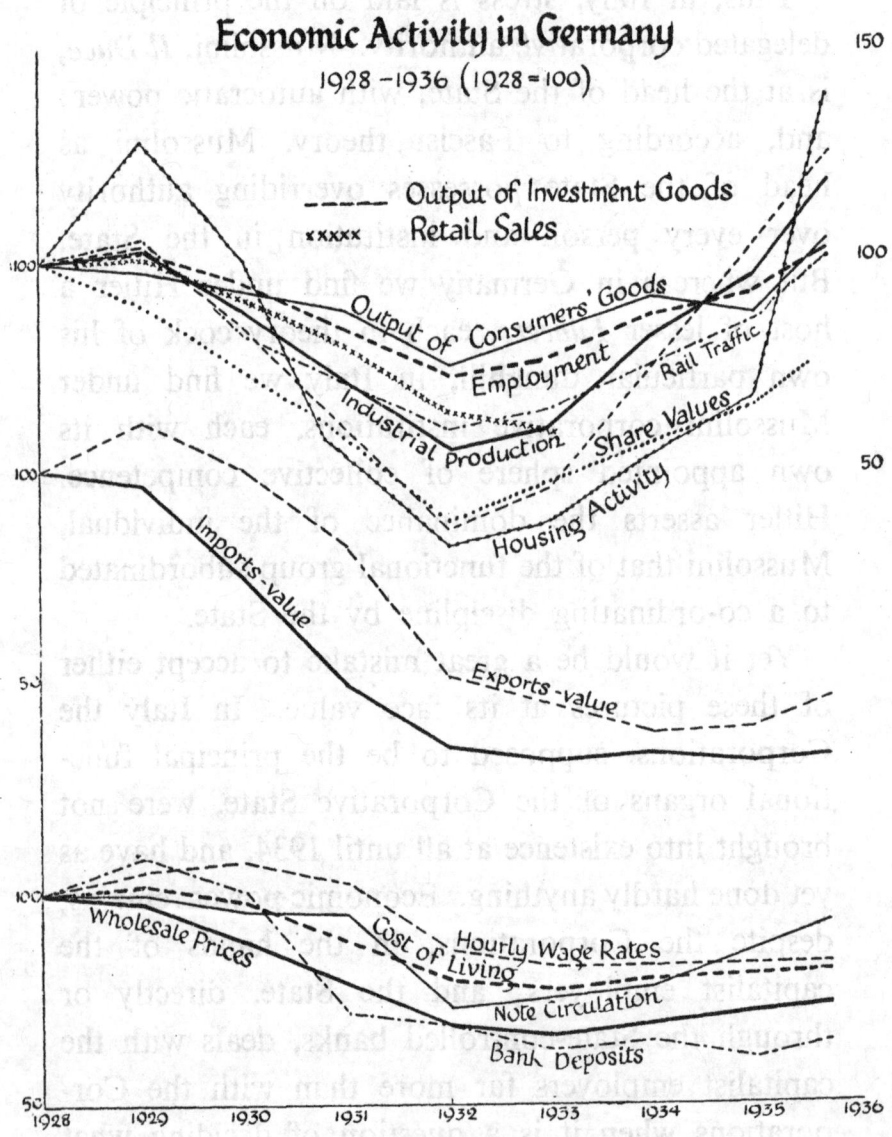

ECONOMIC ACTIVITY IN GERMANY, 1928–1936
(1928—100)

	1929	1930	1931	1932	1933	1934	1935	1936 (Oct.)
Industrial Production	101	87	69	54	61	81	95	114
Output of Investment Goods	103	84	54	35	45	75	102	124
Output of Consumers' Goods	97	91	87	74	80	90	86	102
Employment	101	94	82	72	75	86	91	102
Housing Activity	127	100	46	31	37	52	63	137
Rail Traffic	104	82	69	59	63	76	85	99
Retail Trade Activity	100	92	79	63	60	—	—	—
Net Imports—Value	96	74	48	33	30	32	30	31
Net Exports—Value	111	100	81	50	43	37	38	45
Wholesale Prices	98	89	79	69	67	70	73	74
Cost of Living	102	98	90	80	78	80	81	82
Hourly Wage-rates	105	107	102	86	83	83	83	83
Industrial Share Values	89	71	54	36	46	55	62	74
Note Circulation	100	96	95	73	74	78	86	93
Bank Deposits	108	100	72	69	63	65	61	65

lead various sections of the national economy have in fact very little power over policy. As in Italy direct economic power remains chiefly with the great capitalist interests—wholly so as against the working classes. To the extent to which capitalist powers are restricted, the restriction is due to the great and ever-increasing power of the military chiefs. The capitalists are free to tyrannise over labour; but they must so conduct their industries as to serve the purposes of the war-lords, who represent, far more than in Italy, a distinct power not to be identified with either the Nazi Party or the capitalist interests. German militarism accepts political Fascism as its instrument, just as German capitalism accepts Fascism. But whereas, in Italy, Fascism under Mussolini has so far fairly effectively co-ordinated and reconciled capitalist and militarist aims, in Germany Nazi policy has been repeatedly swung to and fro by the struggle between these contending forces. At one time it seemed as though Dr. Schacht, doubling the parts of Governor of the *Reichsbank* and Minister of Economic Affairs, and holding all the strings of German economic activity in his hands, was destined to become the capitalist dictator of Germany, with Hitler as little more than the figurehead of a quintessentially capitalist State. But latterly the rival influence has asserted itself far more forcibly in the economic field. The German economy has become a war economy, organised for war under the ultimate direction of German militarism. Dr. Schacht retains much power; but General Goering has been put over his head as the supreme co-ordinator of economic policy. Dr. Schacht continues to deal directly and indirectly with the great capitalists who are his friends—directly as Minister, and indirectly through the banks which, now holding a large part of the capital of industry, are in their turn mainly owned by the *Reich*, and under the effective control of the *Reichsbank*.

But Dr. Schacht can co-ordinate industry as the representative of German capitalism only on condition that he uses his authority to carry out a policy which meets the views of the militarists. He is compelled to use his great power over foreign trade and exchange in such ways as will serve the twofold object of strengthening Germany's political hold abroad and of pressing forward the policy of national self-sufficiency which the militarists regard as an indispensable part of the preparation for war. He must use his power over industry to make industry war-conscious and war-equipped, to convert the entire German economy, even in time of peace, into a vast adjunct to the military machine. He must stimulate only those forms of production which will directly strengthen the nation with a view to war, and must subordinate all purely economic considerations to this one supreme object.

Naturally this subjection is not complete, even to-day, though it has gone much further than it had even a few months ago. The capitalists, though they largely share the ambitions and outlook of the militarist leaders, do not passively allow themselves to be diverted from more to less profitable courses. They kick at times, and Dr. Schacht kicks for them: the result is a series of compromises with the militarists continually gaining ground. But, in order that capitalism may be reconciled to serving militarist ends, it has to be bribed. The supreme bribe Nazism offers it is the unrestricted right to exploit defenceless labour.

In view of these large differences in both theory and practice, it is necessary to consider the position of economic planning in the two leading Fascist countries separately, and not as mere variants of a common policy. There are, however, certain features in the economic situation which have exerted a largely similar influence on both countries; and it will be convenient to begin with these.

It is safe to say that in both Italy and Germany State intervention in the economic field has gone a great deal further than it would have gone but for the world crisis. Of course, this is true to some extent of all countries; but among the greater it applies with special force to these two. In both cases the strain of economic troubles has compelled the State to step in in order to save both the financial and the industrial structure from collapse. In both a large part of industry has passed by way of frozen bank advances into the power and virtual ownership of the banks; and in both the banks themselves have had to be reconstructed with State aid, by methods that have made them virtually State agents. In both countries the currency situation has required a rigid control of all foreign exchange operations, administered by the Central Bank on behalf of the State; and this need to safeguard the currency has involved a no less rigid control of imports, by means not only of tariffs but also of numerous quotas, embargoes, and special restrictive trade agreements with other States. In both countries the need to combat unemployment has led to extensive public works policies, and also to the subsidising of private industries in order to persuade them to engage additional labour. In both this policy has involved internal monetary expansion, which has led to increases in the cost of living; and attempts have been made to check these increases by State control of prices. In both countries wages have been deliberately reduced without a corresponding fall in the cost of living; and in both the workers have been continually adjured to tighten their belts in the overmastering interest of the nation. Again, in both countries every effort has been made to expand the production of food, both for military reasons and in order to diminish the need for imports, and also because Fascism and Nazism alike aim at protecting the peasants and the landlords, who have been among their principal supporters, against the catastrophic effects of the fall in world agricultural prices.

Doubtless, some of these things would have been done even if there had been no world economic crisis; but they would certainly have been done with much less intensity. That they have been done for the most part in more extreme ways in Germany than in Italy is only in part due to differences in character between the German and Italian Revolutions: it is also due largely to the greater severity with which the crisis fell upon the advanced, but ill-proportioned, structure of reconstructed Capitalism in post-war Germany.

In Germany, State control over industry had advanced a very long way before the Nazis came to power. In comparison with British, or French, or American Capitalism, the Capitalism of Germany has been, ever since its emergence in the latter part of the nineteenth century, State-fostered and partly planned with the encouragement of the State. Germany has never been a country of *laissez-faire* or economic individualism. Bismarck sought to plan industry, as well as railways, with a view to the might of the German *Reich*; and his trade policy was always a 'planned' compromise between the claims of the Junkers and his desire to foster industrial development. During the war, largely under Walther Rathenau's organising influence, but also under military inspiration, German industry was mobilised for war service far more completely and rigidly than the industries of the Allied countries. Moreover, German law and public opinion have never shared the instinctive hostility to combines and monopolies which has been strong until recently in both British and Latin legal traditions, and in the minds of politicians and voters in Great Britain, France and the United States. To the German, with his belief in order and discipline, it has seemed from the first right that industry should be planned; and cartel organisation, so far from meeting with public hostility, has been deliberately encouraged by the State, which participated in it in respect of public enterprises long before the war.

Now the cartel, which had become before 1914 the typical form of large-scale capitalist enterprise in Germany, stands for a highly developed form of restrictive planning. Like all restrictive agencies, it is fully capable of pursuing a policy of expansion at times, when the going for the profit-makers is good. But it reveals its real nature whenever it has to face a falling market, in its endeavours to hold up prices and to restrict output to 'what the market will bear.' Under the Weimar Republic, as under the pre-war Empire, cartellisation was encouraged, and grew apace; but after 1918, and especially after 1924, the policy of the German Republic was simultaneously to stimulate and strengthen the cartels, even to the extent of making membership compulsory, and to subject them to some sort of State regulation in respect of price-fixing. Till the world crisis this regulation meant little; but as the difficulties of the German economy grew, Governments were compelled to take some action against the marked tendency for the prices of cartellised goods to get out of adjustment with other prices. Under Brüning as Chancellor State regulation was strengthened; and the Nazis inherited a system which already gave the State, in law, wide powers of control over the cartellised section of the German economy.

Before that, the financial crisis of 1931 had compelled the State to make far more drastic incursions into the field of business enterprise. Under pressure of the world depression, which fell with special force on the German economy, banks and big industrial enterprises alike became insolvent, and the *Reich* had to step in with large amounts of fresh working capital in order to save them from collapse. Between 1924 and 1929 Germany had re-built and rationalised her heavy industries at very high capital cost, largely with borrowed money carrying interest at high rates. Domestic capital, which was scarce, was absorbed either in capital construction, or in loans to finance the expansion of exports to Central and Eastern Europe; and working capital had therefore also to be borrowed abroad. The withdrawal of such parts of this capital as its owners were able to retrieve caused an acute financial crisis, accompanied by a rapid deflation of values. Stepping in to avert collapse, the State became virtual owner of a considerable part of the German banking system and of some of the leading industries. The separate banks lost their independence, and came to depend almost completely on the *Reichsbank* and its subsidiaries, as agents of the *Reich* Government; and, as the banks in turn were the virtual owners of many industrial enterprises, the *Reichsbank*, with the Government behind it, acquired control over a very large fraction of the German economic system.

All this had happened before the advent of the Nazis, not because the successive Governments of the *Reich* wished it to happen, but against their will and intention as a necessary measure for preventing sheer economic collapse. It was left for the Nazis, by destroying the Trade Unions and regimenting the workers in the new 'Labour Front', to bring the regulation of working conditions also completely under the authority of the State, which proceeded to use its power for the depression of wages in order to lower costs and increase the competitive power of German industry. But, with the mark maintained at an unchanged value in terms of gold, no wage-cutting could prevent a severe decline in exports. In these circumstances, it was impossible to remain even nominally on gold without drastically curtailing imports. This meant a system of almost absolute protection for many of the products of German industry; and at the same time, as we have seen, almost absolute protection was accorded to German agriculture. It became impossible to import goods into Germany without the permission of the *Reichsbank*, which did not give it easily except for indispensable raw materials or under definite agreements for the mutual exchange of products.

In these ways, both under Brüning and under von Papen and Hitler the German Government built up a structure of economic controls that covered almost every field of business enterprise. But these controls were of no avail in checking the growth of unemployment; for on the whole, except in agriculture, their effects were definitely restrictive, and even the large advances made to banking and industry out of public funds were applied to save existing businesses from collapse and not to stimulate additional enterprise. The growth of unemployment involved a crushing burden on the German system; and, before Hitler's advent to power, Brüning and still more von Papen had been searching for methods of reducing this burden. Von Papen, especially, began that method of stimulating capital investment by tax remissions and postponements which has played so large a part in reviving activity in the heavy industries under the Nazi régime. The *Reich* and the *Reichsbank*, through its subsidiaries, began also to invest heavily in business enterprise in order to finance new constructional work. These investments, in view of the condition of the public finances and of the *Reichsbank's* reserves, could be provided only by inflationary methods; but by means of the rigid control over foreign exchange and imports the external value of the currency was nominally preserved.

These expansionist policies did greatly reduce unemployment, causing an enlargement of production that went much further in the constructional industries than in those supplying consumers' goods. There was a substantial recovery, within these limits; but recovery on these conditions involved a continuance of the most far-reaching forms of public control. Production could be allowed to expand far only in those branches which could proceed without using largely increased supplies of imported materials; and to compensate businesses for the tight hand kept on them by the Government, cartels were given an assurance of the available market by restrictions and positive prohibitions on the launching of new competitive enterprises. Cartels, based on compulsory membership, became more than ever State-regulated monopolies in this or that sphere of production, working at largely State-controlled costs and selling to an increasing extent at State-controlled prices. The State had to strike a balance between allowing the monopolist high profits in order to encourage him to fresh investment in his business, and protecting the consumers, whose incomes were largely State-controlled, from being so exploited by these monopolists as to destroy the market.

Thus there arose in Nazi Germany the caricature of a planned economy based on an extreme form of Economic Nationalism. The State had become virtual owner of a large part of the economic apparatus, and the activity of this apparatus had come to depend to an enormous extent on Government orders for arms and public works, Government subsidies to industry for capital construction, tax remissions and postponements for the same purpose, Government licences to do this or that, Government prohibitions and injunctions, Government regulation of wages so as to keep costs down, and of prices so as to prevent their purchasing power from being utterly eclipsed, Government manipulation of foreign trade and exchange, Government encouragement to agriculture, and last but not least Government-controlled printing of money.

The State machine came to control the economic machine with the heaviest hand ever laid on in any capitalist country. But who controlled the State?

The Nazis came to power as the declared enemies of Big Business, the friends of the 'small man' who was being ground down by the great capitalist trusts, the inveterate enemies of Marxism but the advocates of a *National* Socialism that would put the claims of the whole people far above those of any sectional interest. But actually, having won power with these slogans, the Nazis did nothing against Big Business, with which they had already to a great extent come to terms before power was won. They strengthened the great capitalists, even more than the small, by destroying the Trade Unions; and they promptly made the big business enterprises, under their old capitalist leadership, the chief agents in the execution of their economic policy. Compulsory cartellisation strengthened the great capitalists against the small, just as the N.R.A. did in the United States; and the State-controlled banks, which held industry in their grip, were administered chiefly for the advantage of the big rather than the little debtors. Of the 'small men,' only the peasants benefited by the German 'New Deal'; for the Nazis wanted to make Germany self-sufficient in food supply, and that could not be done without giving the peasant the benefit of high prices for his produce—and besides, what helped the peasants was no less helpful to landlords and creditors in the collection of rents and debts.

In effect, the German situation very well illustrates

the inherent contradictions of a planned capitalist economy. Industrial production increased sharply after the Nazis came to power; but the increase was mainly in capital goods and far less in consumers' goods. More workers were employed; but the standard of living fell. What, however, is the purpose of capital goods, if it be not to enlarge the supply of consumers' goods? It can have but one other purpose—military preparation.

More and more, it did come to serve this purpose. For at this point the militarists began to take a hand; and their grip has been getting firmer ever since. In the latter days of the Weimar Republic, the demand for labour was kept up by 'public works.' Under the Nazis, this policy was intensified; and the public works began to take on a decisively military character. Strategic roads were built in great numbers, and so were aerodromes; and a vast amount of energy was put into the development of aviation. Factories capable of being turned into armament and chemical factories were intensively developed; motor factories were re-equipped; labour camps became more openly places of quasi-military training.

But the aims of the militarists went much further than this. In their view Germany in 1918 was not beaten in the field, but starved into revolution and collapse. It was, therefore, indispensable, in order that Germany might win her war of revenge, to place her in such a position that neither should her civil population be starved into surrender or revolt, nor her armies perish for lack of war material. In order to achieve this immunity, the home production of foodstuffs had at any cost to be greatly increased. In this Herr Darré, the Nazi Minister of Agriculture, was ready enough to aid the militarists, and to join with them in overcoming the opposition of Dr. Schacht and the industrialists, who feared the economic consequences of dearer food. Darré, as the champion of the peasants, helped the military leaders to carry this part of their programme. But it was also necessary to make the country more nearly self-sufficient in essential raw materials, and to use up a part of Germany's scanty supply of foreign exchange in building up stocks of such materials as could not possibly be produced at home. In order to reduce this need to the minimum, an intensive search for home-produced substitutes was begun, and many uneconomic industries, such as the production of oil from coal, were actively fostered.

As these industrial manœuvres meant a lop-sided and uneconomic development of Germany's resources, the attempt to enforce them involved a tough struggle with the capitalists and with their champion, Dr. Schacht. The focus of this struggle came to be the famous German Four-Year Plan—very different in its conception from the Five-Year Plans of the Soviet Union.

The German 'Four-Year Plan of Economic Self-Sufficiency' was proclaimed by Hitler himself at the Nazi Congress in September, 1936. Its announced aim was to make Germany, within four years, able to supply herself completely with all necessary raw materials, without need of imports from abroad. In October, General Goering, who had earlier been put over Dr. Schacht as supreme co-ordinator of German economic policy, was put in charge of the Plan, with power to issue legally binding decrees and administrative orders for its execution. A few days later Goering announced that the Plan would be carried out under six heads —production of raw materials, distribution of raw materials, supply of labour, agricultural production, price-control, and foreign exchange regulation. It was stated that Goering would consult with Schacht over the last of these—a further narrowing of the former capitalist dictator's recognised sphere of influence. There followed the appointment of a price-controller, Herr Wagner, instructed to prevent prices from rising as a result of the Plan; and a little later Goering issued a new code of regulations which prevented employers from competing for the supply of skilled labour, compelled them to train a larger number of apprentices, and virtually subjected the entire skilled labour force in Germany to a system of supervision and regimentation very similar to that which existed during the late war.

What the German Four-Year Plan means, in terms of the standards of living of the German people, can be realised by anyone who has studied recent German official documents. For example, the virtually official *Institut für Konjuncturforschung* has recently issued an elaborate memorandum telling the citizens what types of food they may consume, and what they are to avoid, in the interests of the nation. In this highly instructive document, the first emphasis is laid on reduced consumption of all products of animal origin, with the exception of fish and rabbits. Each hectare of soil, it is pointed out, can be made to yield a far larger food value if it is used to produce vegetable products than if animals are fed upon it. One hectare under potatoes, it is calculated, gives twenty times as great a caloric value as one used for producing beef; and one hectare under wheat is nearly ten times as productive in this sense. Accordingly, the German people is adjured to 'change over to a diet which prefers plant products, such as potatoes, vegetables and sugar, rather than animal products.' Animal fat, being hardest of all to produce in adequate quantities, is to be specially avoided; but consumption of vegetable fats is also to be kept down to the minimum, because the ingredients have largely to be imported. Fruit consumption, again, is to be kept down, wherever it creates a demand for imports.

Special stress is laid by the *Institut* on the cheapness of the diet which it proposes, as well as on its contribution to national *autarkie*. On this score margarine is greatly preferable to butter; but as both have to be imported consumption of both must be reduced. The richer classes can have butter, because it can be largely imported on barter terms. The poor cannot afford butter; and they must not substitute margarine, because its ingredients can be bought abroad only for cash.

Not content with these general proposals for a change in the national diet the *Institut* goes on to prescribe an elaborate series of seasonal variations in the people's consumption, in accordance with fluctuations in the available supply. The German is told exactly what he may eat each month, as well as what to avoid. And he is provided with a complete schedule of the foods of which, under the Nazi plan, total consumption is to be decreased, kept stable, or increased by way of making up for the deprivation of the tabooed substances. Thus, he must eat less beef, veal, bacon, butter, lard, margarine, table oils and fats, imported vegetables, and fatty cheese. He may keep unchanged his consumption of pork, eggs, game and poultry, bread, rice, cocoa, most fruit, peas, beans, lentils, milk and honey. But he may consume more potatoes—these are given pride of place—sugar, jam, home-produced cheese and vegetables, sago, butter-milk, fish and rabbits. That is, if he can get more; for even of

FASCIST 'PLANNING': GERMANY—ITALY

some of these products the supply is at present short.

What must be the outcome of these changes in diet, if they become effective, on the health of the people? In effect, the German nation is being asked to live almost wholly on calorific foods, with only the scantiest provision either for body-building or for protection against disease. It is being urged, as a measure of national preparation for war—for that is what it comes to—to place itself at a standard of nutrition which would put it definitely on a level with the most impoverished section of the British people, according to Sir John Orr's classification of it into nutritional groups. For it will not escape the reader's notice that the foods possessing body-building or protective value of which the consumption is not strongly discouraged are for the most part so expensive as to be well beyond the reach of the great majority of the people.

Especially is the recommended diet likely to have disastrous reactions on the health of children and nursing mothers. But it is also calamitously ill-balanced in relation to ordinary adult needs. Calories indeed it may yield in sufficient quantities, if the German people can be induced to live mainly on potatoes—though it is not clear what is to happen when the potato harvest, which is notoriously variable, happens to fail. Presumably, if that occurs, the Germans are to be reduced to the plight of the Irish cottagers in the Hungry

Forties—a plight which, it will be remembered, forced Peel to abolish the Corn Laws.

These dietary particulars have been given at some length because they bring out, more clearly than anything else, the human consequences of what Nazi Germany is now attempting to do. The German standard of living is being beaten down by two main forces—the diversion of manpower from producing consumable goods to rearmament, and the curtailment of imports as a means both to rearmament and to that national self-sufficiency which is regarded as indispensable for war. The Germans must live wretchedly, first because their incomes will not allow them to live any better, but also secondly because they must live already after the manner of a beleaguered city.

Compare what this means with the Russian experience during the early years of the Soviets. The Russian people had to fare even worse than the Germans—even a great deal worse. But their fate was for the time unavoidable, and the controllers of the Soviet economy were straining every nerve to provide a way of escape by expanding home production—with reasonable hope of making the standard of living higher within a decade or so than it had ever been before. The present German measures hold out no such hope for the future. For, while it may be possible to raise home production of foodstuffs above the existing level, it is as certain as anything can be that the German people cannot live even tolerably well if it attempts to live almost exclusively on the produce of German agriculture. A decent standard of living and a balanced nutrition imperatively require importation on a large scale.

The German plan, therefore, threatens the German people with devastating malnutrition, not merely for a few years, but for as long as it lasts. It may be answered that it cannot be meant to last; and, of course, it is not. But—and this is the point—it cannot possibly be ended by the success of the plan. If it is to be regarded as a temporary measure, that is only because it is a war measure. The way of escape from malnutrition which the Nazis are holding out to the people is victory in war, which will place vast food-producing areas at the service of the German economy.

The food campaign is only one aspect of the Nazi plan. The Germans' heads are hardly less full of their projects for the mass-production of synthetic textiles, synthetic petrol, synthetic rubber—synthetic substitutes for every material that cannot be found or produced at home. Now, the trouble about most of these substitutes is that, in the existing condition of technique, they are either, like oil, very expensive to produce, or like synthetic rubber, both expensive and very lacking in durability. As far as they enter into consumption, they involve a serious rise in the cost of living. But the German working and middle classes have no margin of incomes wherewith to face such a rise. They are hard enough put to it already in making both ends meet.

Accordingly, both the food plan and the materials plan represent additional explosive forces in the German internal situation. On the one hand, the military leaders doubtless desire to avoid war until their war preparations, including their preparations for *autarkie*, are nearer completion. But on the other hand, it is impossible to believe that the privations which are being inflicted on the mass of the people, and the further privations which are now threatened, will not very soon set up an acute condition of internal nervous strain. It is true that a whole people can almost incredibly tighten its belt—the Russians have shown that. But it can hardly tighten it cheerfully to so extreme a point as Nazi policy demands without either being driven on by a feverish war-enthusiasm or reacting strongly against the regime. The Four-Year Plan looks like polarising the nation—driving some of it towards the extremes of bellicosity and others, who dare for the time only grumble in secret, to a more intense hatred of the dictatorship.

Doubtless, the Nazi leaders are alive to the danger of this second reaction. As far and as fast as they can, they will ease the situation by means of barter arrangements with foreign countries for the exchange of foodstuffs for German manufactures. Hence Dr. Schacht's recent journeyings; hence the lively preoccupation of the German technical journals with the production statistics and possibilities of South-Eastern Europe. But it is realised that barter arrangements cannot easily be pushed much further than they have been already, at any rate under the existing political conditions. Hence, again, the growing belief, in party circles, that successful warfare offers the only way of escape.

In December, 1936, Col. Thomas, a leading official at the German War Ministry, was writing of the Four-Year Plan as 'a result of our thinking along the lines of war economy,' and was stressing the need for a complete regimentation and discipline of the entire body of workers as an integral part of the Plan.

All this shows how completely Nazi Germany has now become a State planned and planning for war. The entire balance of the German economy now rests on military preparation. If that prop were knocked away, the whole edifice would be bound to collapse.

Germany remains, however, fundamentally capitalist, though her capitalism is now twisted to serve military objectives. She is still under the necessity, if her militarist policy is to be carried out, of making it pay the capitalists to act upon it. For the one thing Nazism dare not face is a recrudescence of unemployment; and that can be prevented only by making it profitable for the capitalists to employ a sufficient amount of labour.

If, however, the *entrepreneurs* are to be encouraged

to employ additional labour, the costs of production must be kept down, and they must be allowed a sufficient prospect of profit to make the additional employment worth their while. Low wages and high prices seem, from this point of view, to be the only available cures for economic depression. They encourage *entrepreneurs* to make increased investment and thereby to employ more workers. But if the additional employment is to be made possible by reducing wages, who is to consume the additional products which the enlarged apparatus of production enables the employers to place on the market? To some extent the owners of industry can consume these products themselves, or the State can acquire them for public purposes, including the provision of increased military supplies. But if the State is to buy the additional products, it will have to pay for them; and this it can do only by raising taxation, and so restricting other kinds of demand, or by borrowing, which has for the time the same effect, if the borrowings are drawn from real savings, or finally by creating more *fiat* money, which will also restrict demand in other fields by diluting the general purchasing power at the command of the members of the community. What the State spends in such a case must be directly or indirectly subtracted from the purchasing power of its citizens.

On the other hand, if the recipients of the enlarged profits spend their additional receipts on home-produced consumable goods no crisis need arise. But will they? It is most unlikely that they will, as long as high profits are to be had from additional investment. But if the demand for consumers' goods does not expand, how can investment continue to be profitable? It can so continue only as long as the State continues to provide the demand, by orders for public works, munitions of war, and whatever other things the State can provide the means of consuming. Consequently, the State must continue indefinitely to provide an artificial demand, if the whole edifice is not to collapse.

But cannot a remedy be found in raising wages, and so enabling the consumers to buy more goods? Hardly; for the effect of raising costs of production will be to narrow the area of profitability, and thus cause a contraction of employment. If the State then expands its public works, or its demand for armaments, in order to offset this contraction, it will be able to raise the required funds only by inflation; for the lowering of profits will have narrowed the surplus available for taxation. The State is in a dilemma; for if once it does set out on the financing of public works by sheer inflation in order to counteract a fall in profits and employment, the process becomes cumulative, and can only end in economic crisis and collapse.

Accordingly, the high-wage remedy is not open; and there remains only the alternative of securing that the high profits of industry shall be diverted to the construction of public works and armaments, since they cannot be used for making undemanded additional supplies of consumable goods. The Germans have sought to apply this remedy. They have forbidden joint stock concerns to distribute more than a limited rate of dividend, and compelled them to lend their surplus profits to the State, which uses them to finance armaments, subsidies, and other expenses involved in its militarist policy. In this way, the demand for the products of the constructional industries is maintained, and unemployment kept within bounds.

Any expansionist policy, however, is bound to create a demand for additional imports. The low level of wage-costs will to some extent facilitate exports, and so help to provide means of paying for these imports, especially if exporting industries are so cartellised as to be able to make effective price-discriminations between home and foreign customers, selling exports at marginal prices while keeping up prices in the domestic market. But Germany is seriously handicapped in following this policy—though she does follow it to the best of her power—by the high external value of her currency. Hence the acceptance of payment for 'additional exports' in various kinds of 'blocked' and 'registered' marks given in payment for imports. Hence, too, the numerous trade agreements which Germany has made with other countries, so as to purchase their goods by way of a regulated barter for German exports.

It remains true that, in face of the condition of Germany's export trade, total imports cannot be expanded. But some imports must expand, at any rate until the Four-Year Plan has done its work, if the constructional expansion and the process of intensive re-armament are not to be brought to a stand. In order to make this possible, other imports must be cut to the bone, and every effort must be made to provide home-produced substitutes, even at high cost, for types of goods such as rubber and petrol, which were previously brought in from abroad. This process of substitution will, incidentally, call for new capital construction, and thus provide outlets for some of the investment that must take place if the expansion of economic activity is to be maintained. It will also involve, and be held to justify, a very high level of agricultural protection.

The position, then, of the German economy to-day is that internal expansion is being kept up, in face of a very low standard of living, by intensive rearmament, and by the stimulus to investment afforded by active substitution of home-produced goods for imports. But this process is costly and difficult. It involves producing at high real costs, despite low wages, what could be produced better abroad. It involves the State in constant borrowing, to which the only alternative is a resort to open inflation. It depends on keeping the standard of living low, both because a rise in it would create an imperative demand for additional imports, and because the burden on the public funds can be kept within manageable limits only by offering the employer the inducement of low wages as a means to high profits. But the employer must not spend these high profits on imports, or be allowed to hoard them; and as the field of consumers' demand is limited by the lowness of wages, the State must borrow the excess profits, and spend them for 'public purposes.'

This position is bound to be highly unstable. It can last as long as the demand for imports can be kept, by increasing substitution, within manageable limits, and as long as the State can continue to find 'public purposes' sufficient to keep up the total volume of industrial activity. But the second necessity has the very grave effect of giving the State a positive economic incentive to more and more intensive re-armament, which is a convenient way of absorbing labour in 'public works,' and also keeps alive a nationalist spirit which inclines the people to submit more tamely to a low standard of life.

I am not saying that, under these conditions, it is impossible for the German standard of living to rise at all above the low point to which it has fallen in the course of the crisis. It can rise to some extent, where the German economy can adapt itself to conditions of *autarkie* without serious economic loss. As the efficiency of production rises, the purchasing power of wages can partially recover; but the rise in real wages must be less than the rise in real efficiency if the stimulus of high profits is to be preserved, and the State to be relieved of part of the burden of employing the people. The Nazis do not want the standard of living to be low: they would gladly raise it if they could as a means of consolidating their power. But they cannot raise it, without causing the economic system to collapse, until and unless they can reconcile *autarkie* with both high profits and a higher efficiency of production. As *autarkie*, in its earlier stages at any rate, is calculated to lower efficiency, this confronts them with a sufficiently formidable task.

Such is the German 'planned economy' of Hitler and the militarists. It bears little resemblance to the economic plans which Nazi theorists, such as Feder and Strasser, used to formulate for popular consumption before the party came to power. It shares with these earlier plans little more than an aggressively nationalist outlook and a determination to prevent unemployment from reaching the formidable total which brought the Weimar Republic to its ruin. Nazi policy remains nationalist and expansionist; but it retains not a trace of Socialism or anti-capitalism, which used to be a powerful ingredient of it in earlier days. So far from attacking Big Business, it makes the great industrialists and their cartels its leading instruments in industry. So far from raising wages and lowering profits, it makes the offer of low wages as a means to high profits the pivot of its policy of expanding private employment. So far from distributing purchasing power among the people, it concentrates it in the hands of the great employers and the State. And, so far from socialising large-scale industry, it is making every possible effort to re-vitalise private enterprise, and to get back into the hands of the industrialists those bankrupt properties which the crisis compelled the State to take under its control.

A 'planned economy' of this sort has for its object not the securing of the highest possible all-round standard of living, which is the sole rational end of economic action, but only its own maintenance for quite other ends. The object of German 'planning' is not to make the people better off, but to enable the Nazis to remain in power, and to uphold those propertied interests which have allied themselves with the Nazis for the defeat of Socialism. Of course, the Nazis and even their capitalist backers would be quite pleased if they could secure their own ends and at the same time make the people richer; but, like capitalists everywhere, they seek national welfare only as a by-product of their own interest. There is accordingly nothing in common between Nazi 'planning' and the planning which aims at human welfare; for real economic planning, as we have seen, must be thought of as relative to the one truly worthwhile economic end—the greatest welfare of the greatest number.

Moreover, German 'planning,' apart from its inherent instability and its uneconomic character, is essentially explosive. A nation which is, from the economic standpoint, wasting a large part of its substance on arming for war is bound before long to endeavour to turn its armaments to profit. The more it impoverishes itself internally in order to become formidable in a military sense, the greater is its urge to expand outwards. It needs expansion for two reasons—first because it must justify its huge military expenditure to the people whom it condemns to poverty, and secondly because those who deify force are certain to believe that force can be made to yield an economic return.

This belief is seen most clearly in the shifting gospel of the Nazi leaders. They dream at one time of a drive to the east and south—a drive which will make them the masters of the Ukraine and establish their economic power throughout Eastern Europe. At another time they dream of a southward drive to the Mediterranean and the Near East—of economic dominion over the Balkans and Asia Minor and all the lands of Central Europe. But most of all they dream just now of colonies, of a colonial Empire that will enable them to surpass the wealth of Britain, and provide them, within a self-contained economic unit, with markets for further exports and supplies of cheap materials based on the exploitation of native labour. Empire has paid Britain richly, they argue. Why should it not pay Germany?

The answer must be that, for the Germans, the road to Empire runs through world war; and the wars of to-day are destructive and ruinous infinitely beyond the wars of the past. At the very most, the chance of making a profit out of modern war is exceedingly small. It is possible only if victory is swift and crushing, so that the enemy is put out of action before there has been time for the destruction to reach serious dimensions. But is such a victory likely? To bank on it is surely a desperate gamble. Yet that is what Germany appears to be doing, as far as her conduct is capable of being rationally interpreted at all.

When we turn from Germany to Italy—from Nazism to Fascism properly so called—we encounter both resemblances and differences. In Italy, as in Germany, much stress has been laid on the need for economic self-sufficiency, though Italy, on account of the deficiency of vital natural resources, is much less in a position than Germany both to achieve this and to develop towards a more advanced type of industrialism. There is the same problem of paying for necessary imports out of the proceeds of exports, in view of the depressing effect on exports of an overvalued currency. Italy, like Germany, had been driven off the gold standard in fact long before she departed from it in name, and had been compelled to resort to similar methods of centralised control over foreign exchange and drastic limitation of imports by means of quotas and other restrictions. In Italy, as in Germany, wages have been drastically cut down in order to enlarge the area of profitability for the employers, and so lessen unemployment; and the State, even before the great drive towards armaments which preceded the Abyssinian War, had stepped in with large schemes of public works and financial help towards the expansion and re-equipment of industry in order to keep the constructional trades employed. In Italy, even more than in Germany, these measures have been accompanied by compulsory reductions in prices, in order to check the undue contraction of demand and prevent the cost of living from soaring far beyond the means of the wage-earners. In Italy, as in Germany, the crisis has compelled the State to reorganise and re-finance the banks, and the banks, as agents of the State, to play a large part in the control and reorganisation of embarrassed industries.

Italy, however, is far less industrialised than Germany, and less dependent on foreign trade in normal times. Her dependence on foreign supplies of industrial materials is greater than Germany's; but these materials bulk less in her national economy. She can therefore reconstruct herself with less profound economic transformation to a rela-

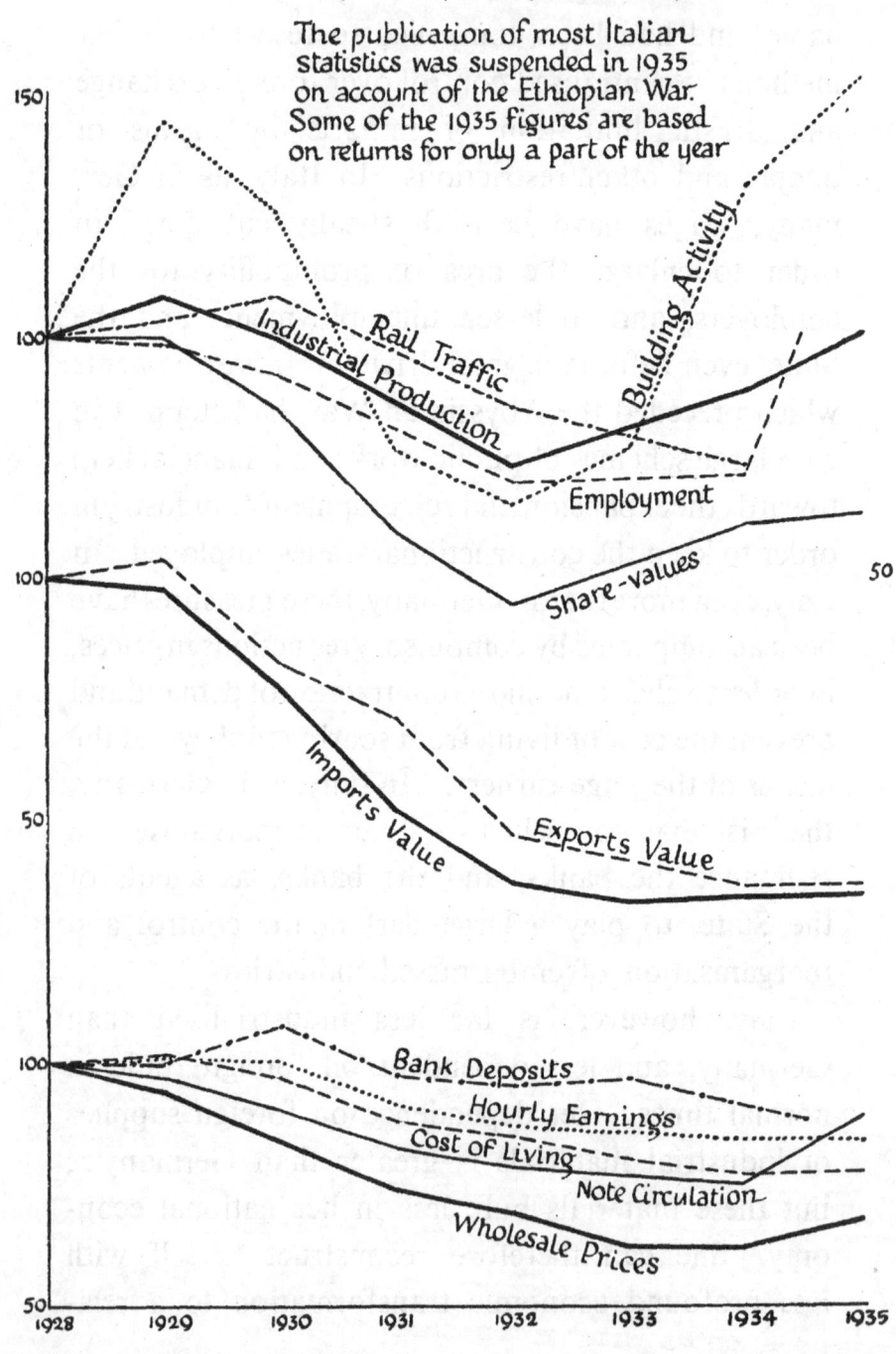

ECONOMIC ACTIVITY IN ITALY, 1928–1935
(1928 = 100)

	1929	1930	1931	1932	1933	1934	1935*
Industrial Production	109	100	85	73	81	88	100 (June)
Building Activity	145	127	77	66	77	129	152
Rail Freight Traffic	104	109	99	86	78	73	—
Employment	100	93	81	71	71	72	100 (June)
Unemployment	93	131	226	310	314	297	188
Net Imports—Value	99	79	53	38	34	35	35
Net Exports—Value	105	83	71	47	41	36	36
Wholesale Prices	95	85	74	70	63	62	68
Cost of Living	102	98	89	85	81	77	78
Wages—Hourly Earnings	102	101	92	88	86	84	84
Industrial Share Values	100	86	60	45	52	61	63
Note Circulation	97	91	83	79	77	76	89
Bank Deposits	101	108	98	96	97	93	89 (June)

* First three-quarters of 1935. Most statistics were thereafter suspended on account of the Ethiopian War.

tively self-sufficient system, though reconstruction on these lines is bound to slow down her industrial development over a wide field. Italy, like Germany, has tried in part to meet her unemployment problem by intensive military preparation; but her public works have been less industrial than Germany's, and have been concentrated more largely on land reclamation and improvement and the building of roads. Her total unemployment problem, thanks to her more agricultural structure, has been less heavy than Germany's; and, accordingly the Fascists have not been driven so far as the Nazis in pledging the credit of the State in order to get the unemployed back to work. This is not to say that Italy's unemployment problem has been of no account: far from it. Unemployment had been, and remained, up to the time of the Abyssinian War, very severe among the industrial workers. But in the nature of the case even widespread industrial unemployment produces less devastating social consequences in a largely agricultural country.

Stress has been laid already on the distinction between the 'corporative' aspirations of Mussolini and the principle of personal authority which is emphasised in Nazi Germany. Despite the failure to endow the Italian Corporations with clearly defined functions or extensive powers, this difference is more than skin-deep. Mussolini, as autocratic as Hitler and much cleverer, is far more than the

Nazi *Führer* the real driving force behind the State. And, though both men are under the influence of a nationalistic megalomania that leads to an absurd and pernicious emphasis on military glory, in economic attitude there is a real distinction between them. Hitler is *par excellence* the *petit bourgeois* upholder of class inequality and personal property claims, hating all forms of Socialism that threaten to make him the equal of the class below him and full of snobbish reverence for class differences. Mussolini appears to be devoid of these qualities. He is the 'boss' who has graduated in the school of Socialism, and his experience has left him no respecter of men. He repudiates equality, because he deems men unequal, and equates rights with mights. But, though he upholds private property and maintains the capitalist system, he is far more determined than the Nazis to make capitalists and other property-owners into feudatories of the Fascist State. Their rights depend on their functions, and are conditional on due performance of function. Mussolini might well pursue in the end a sort of bastard 'Socialism' without class equality, if the present adjustment of forces in Italy broke down. And even now he is enough of a Syndicalist, if not a Socialist, to have a hankering after associative rather than personal leadership and control in all that part of Society which, according to Fascist-Hegelian theory, constitutes the social mechanism subordinate to the essentially spiritual overlordship of the State itself.

In the State, Mussolini means to be *Il Duce*. But he has no taste for minor *Duces*. He prefers Corporations, though he does not yet see his way to endow them with real life.

This difference is illustrated by the different position of the one recognised party in the two leading Fascist States. The Italian Fascist Party is more like the Communist Party in the U.S.S.R. than it is like the Nazi Party in Germany. For it is, and the Nazi Party is not a real governing instrument. The Fascist Grand Council, under Mussolini, does rule Italy; and the Corporations are carefully built up under the leadership of tried party members responsible to the party. There is real discussion of policies within the Fascist Party, and the party members do count in its deliberations. On the other hand, nothing in Germany since the Nazi seizure of power has been so remarkable as the falling away of the Nazi Party. Active Nazis have no doubt still wide powers of private persecution and aggrandisement, though even these have been less since the suppression of the S.A. leaders in 1934. But the Nazi Party, as a party, plays practically no part in the formulation of German policy. It is hard to say who does rule Germany to-day—exactly how power is apportioned between, say, Hitler, the Junkers and the *Reichswehr*, Thyssen and Dr. Schacht, though it is clear enough that of late the authority of the *Reichswehr* has very rapidly increased; but the mere list of competitors is enough to show that, wherever power does in fact reside, it is not in the Nazi Party as an organised whole. How indeed could it be?—for the Nazi Party never had a policy, only a technique for the conquest of political power.

It has often been said that there is no Fascist policy in Italy either; and it is undoubtedly true that the Fascist Party came to power with barely the rudiments of a programme. Less self-contradictory than the Nazis, they avoided contradiction largely by saying nothing on most of the real issues. They are still largely without a policy; for the achievement of the Corporative State remains for the most part rather a verbal ideal than a policy actually pursued. Nevertheless, the Fascist Party has vitality enough, under Mussolini's leadership, not to let the control slip from its hands. If its members knew what they wanted, they would have far more chance of getting it than Röhm and his followers ever had.

In the sphere of economic planning, however, there is not a great deal that either Mussolini or the Fascist Party can do. The country, as Mussolini himself has often declared, is unsuitable for intensive capitalist development under present conditions, and must remain largely agricultural. Industrially, it must rest content mainly with the lighter trades; and these call less for the more spectacular kinds of rationalisation than the heavy industries which predominate in the German economy. There are large-scale capitalist enterprises in

Italy, notably in the motor trade and other branches of light engineering; and it is significant that Italy's greatest industrialist, Pirelli, has been throughout Mussolini's principal economic adviser. But large-scale industry occupies a relatively small place in the national life; and there are still many trades carried on by means of very small-scale enterprise. Such types of industry cannot be easily planned; for they depend largely on local markets, and produce very varied goods. Agriculture, despite small-scale operation, can be planned to a somewhat greater extent, wherever it produces for a wide market. But even here 'planning' means as yet little more than regulation of imports, *plus* land reclamation and financial help to farmers designed to induce increased supplies.

It is often said, doubtless with truth, that the Italian railways are far better run under Fascism than they were before; and this may be taken as typical of a tuning-up which has been applied, by means of Fascist discipline, to many types of enterprise. The banks have been reorganised on more efficient lines; and better provision has been made, after the liquidation of the failures brought on by the crisis, for the financing of small-scale industrial, as well as agricultural, enterprise. But these things do not add up to make an economic plan. Italy, far more than Nazi Germany, remains a planless economy, even in the widest sense that can be given to the notion of planning.

In fact, the whole attitude of Fascism is inconsistent with economic planning, in the sense in which it exists in the U.S.S.R., or in any sense in which it is really economic at all. For Fascism, all the world over, is essentially uneconomic. It came to power, subsidised by the great capitalists and reinforced by the small property-owners, as an instrument of force for suppressing Socialism and keeping capitalism in being despite its demonstrated inability to serve the fundamental economic purpose of putting the means of production to effective use for the satisfaction of human needs. Its purpose was thus anti-economic and anti-rational. It could not, however, have sustained itself long in power on the basis of a mere negation of Socialism. It had to proclaim a positive purpose of its own, distinct from the purposes of its capitalist paymasters; for these had no power to hold the loyalty of the people. It found its answer in the gospel of force, of nationalist militarism armed for world conquest.

This gospel involved, if it was to become the real objective of policy, a subordination of even capitalist economic ends to militaristic methods. It meant that capitalism, having conquered Socialism within, had to harness itself to the war machine; and this capitalism, though it stood out at times, was on the whole prepared to do as long as the Fascist dictators would keep the workers in subjection to it and allow them to make profits out of the preparation for war. In Italy, where both economic capitalism and militarism were relatively weak, the war gospel became directly the gospel of the Fascist party without any internal struggle, and Mussolini retained his leadership as the War Lord of the Italian nation. In Germany the course of things was somewhat different; for both capitalism and militarism were strong and independent forces capable of defying and contending for the mastery of the Nazi Party. At first, after the Nazi Revolution, capitalism seemed dominant in the economic sphere, and Schacht the arbiter of economic affairs. But the growth of the militarist spirit carried with it the emergence of the *Reichswehr* as the real controller of Germany, and the Nazi Party became more and more in effect the prisoner of the military leaders. This carried with it, in due course, the domination of the economic life of the country by the militarists. For the Germans are nothing if not thorough; and they have, moreover, a national addiction to discipline. Capitalism in Germany found itself caught up in the march towards world war; and, as German Fascism is the natural leader of the Fascist impulse in all lesser countries, Fascism became everywhere the exponent of an insane gospel of brute force. Whither Fascism is leading the world, who shall say? But assuredly it is not leading towards an orderly planning of the economic life of nations, or towards the best utilisation of the technical resources of production in the service of the common man.

CHAPTER IV

AMERICAN 'PLANNING'—THE NEW DEAL

IT is inevitable that in any consideration of the possibilities of a planned capitalist economy, men's thoughts should turn to recent developments in the United States. For America had provided, before the advent of President Roosevelt, by far the largest example in the world of the working of an entirely unplanned capitalist economy. This economy had been able, because of the vast natural resources at its disposal, and of the immense attractive power which the possibility of exploiting them had exerted upon immigrants from all parts of the world, to develop with extraordinary speed, caring very little whether the method of growth was orderly or chaotic. The American business man, whether he was a large-scale *entrepreneur* or a small farmer or private employer, had been far too busy gathering in the fruits of an almost automatic expansion to give much attention to the future, and American politicians and the American public, under the influence of the so-called 'prosperity psychology,' had done little or nothing to control or to direct the vast forces in whose productivity they had been able to share. Consequently in the United States, up almost to the present time, the business man has been on top and the politician a long way behind. And, even apart from this, the American Constitution, drafted at a time before the problems of a capitalist economy had seriously emerged, had with its insistence on the rights of the individual and the limitations of the public power—to say nothing of the separation of powers between legislature, executive and judiciary, or of that other separation between Federal and State authorities—made strongly against the effectiveness of such few attempts as had been instituted to set up any form of collective regulation over economic affairs.

It is true enough that the United States, more than any other country, had taken a prominent part in legislation directed against trusts, and that the very word 'trust,' as a business term, together with its correlative 'trust-busting,' comes from the United States. The large-scale organisation of American business led inevitably to the emergence of great combines with at times powerful tendencies towards monopoly. But in accordance with the individualist principles of the American Constitution public action against these combines had taken, until the advent of the New Deal, mainly the line of endeavouring to break them up or to prevent their emergence, and seldom that of endeavouring to regulate and control them, as Germany did from the outset with her cartels and syndicates. It is true that monopolies were necessarily recognised and subjected to forms of public control in the spheres of transportation and other public utilities, and that the Federal Trade Commission had attempted to distinguish between price-controlling monopolies and agreements for checking 'unfair' competition; but it remained broadly true that the American courts had taken up a strong line against combination in most of its forms.

For whereas, in Great Britain, it is entirely lawful for a group of capitalist *entrepreneurs* to enter into an agreement for the regulation of output or the maintenance of fixed or minimum prices, in the United States such practices had fallen definitely under the ban of the courts, acting in part under the common law, but also, since 1890, under the Sherman Anti-Trust Act, which was further strengthened by the Clayton Act of 1913. Until the N.R.A. Codes were introduced, it was definitely unlawful for *entrepreneurs* to combine to raise or fix prices, or to create monopolistic conditions; and on a number of occasions attempts to evade the ban by creating a holding company or 'trust,' in the strict sense, had been disallowed by the courts, and the integrated bodies ordered to be broken up again into their component elements. This does not of course mean that trusts and monopolies were unknown or uncommon in the United States: indeed, a large part of the ingenuity of corporation

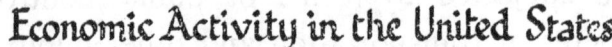

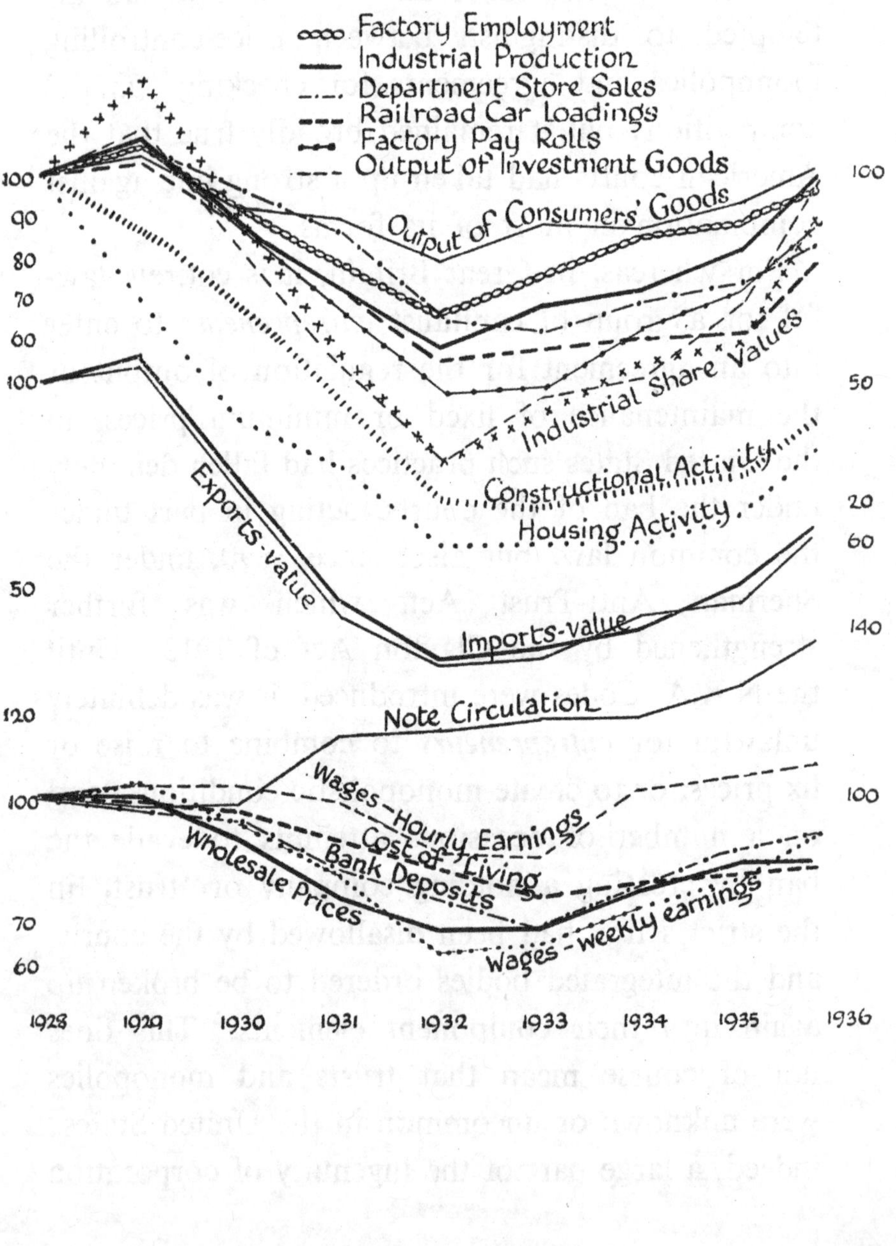

ECONOMIC ACTIVITY IN THE UNITED STATES, 1928–1936
(1928 = 100)

	1929	1930	1931	1932	1933	1934	1935	1936 (Oct.)
Industrial Production	107	87	73	58	68	71	81	98
Output of Investment Goods	109	79	52	30	45	50	69	98
Output of Consumers' Goods	104	91	89	79	87	86	92	100
Building Activity, Total	87	68	47	21	19	24	27	40
Housing Activity	69	40	29	10	9	10	17	33
Rail Goods Traffic	103	89	73	54	56	60	61	82
Factory Employment	106	93	78	66	73	84	87	96
Department Store Sales	103	94	85	64	62	69	73	83
Net Imports—Value	106	76	51	32	35	40	50	63
Net Exports—Value	103	75	47	31	33	42	45	62
Wholesale Prices	99	89	75	67	68	77	83	84
Cost of Living	100	96	87	79	76	79	81	83
Hourly Earnings	102	102	98	86	85	101	104	107
Weekly Earnings	102	93	81	62	64	73	80	90
Factory Payrolls	107	87	66	46	48	62	70	87
Note Circulation	98	98	114	115	118	118	126	136
Bank Deposits	97	93	81	73	68	79	86	90 (June)

lawyers had been devoted to devising methods of combination that the law would be unable to touch. It does, however, mean that the emphasis in the United States had been far more on the formation of huge financially integrated corporations, which became by unification legal persons in the eyes of the courts, and might thus escape the ban, than on trade associations or cartels such as existed in Germany and Great Britain. It also means that the emphasis had been less on price-fixing and restriction of output than on the acquisition of differential advantages by the control of raw materials and means of transportation and of the distributive agencies through which commodities reach the consumers.

In these circumstances, combination between financially independent firms had in the United States taken primarily the line of common agreements for the standardisation and specialisation of output, for the pooling of information. and for the exertion of political pressure over tariffs and other forms of trade regulation; and there had been, save where the greater part of the market was controlled by a single financially unified concern, comparatively little attempt to fix selling prices or output. Undoubtedly, an important further cause of this had been the very rapid expansion, until recently, of the total size of the American market, which for the most part meant that there was little temptation, save in the recurrent periods of recession, to adopt restrictive practices, because it was more profitable as a rule to take advantage of the opportunities for reducing costs by the expansion of sales.

The great American recession of 1929 and the following years fundamentally altered this situation. There appeared to be, in most industries, a great redundancy of productive capacity over market demand; and there was a general fear that competition between producers would lead to an entire collapse of prices. Accordingly, *entrepreneurs* began for the first time to feel seriously the restrictions imposed on them by the Anti-Trust laws, and to clamour for the right, within the law, to enter into open agreements for the regulation of output and prices. The Government, they pointed out, had for some time been deliberately intervening, through the Federal Farm Board and other agencies, in order to raise or hold up the prices of agricultural products. Why should not they be given a corresponding right to regulate industrial prices, and to plan industrial output in closer relation to the actual conditions of the market?

Just as the Agricultural Adjustment Act extended much further than the Government's measures for the maintenance of prices and the enforced restriction of agricultural output, so the N.R.A. swept away for the time being the obstacles interposed by the Anti-Trust Laws, and allowed the American manufacturers to regulate output and prices to their hearts' content. The Government did, indeed, maintain a power of veto over the decisions of the Code Authorities set up under the N.R.A.; but these authorities were, to all intents and purposes, mostly employers' associations given full legal recognition and compulsory powers, and their sheer number and the complexity of the Codes they drew up made it quite impossible for the improvised N.R.A. Administration to exercise any effective control over their doings, even if such control had been really part of the President's policy—which it was not.

Accordingly, the restrictive trust practices already common in Europe developed apace in America in 1933 and 1934 under the auspices of the N.R.A. There was indeed, as a part of the N.R.A. machine, a rudimentary organ of control supposed to represent the consumers; but this had both little power and an impossible task, in face of the multiplicity of codes and the desire of the Administration to minimise interference with the 'self-government' of the various industries. The N.R.A. Codes were therefore for a time effective in many cases in raising prices and restricting supplies—far more effective than similar capitalist organisations in other countries, because the United States had leapt straight from prohibiting to positively encouraging and enforcing on reluctant minorities of employers such practices as were designed to bring

AMERICAN 'PLANNING'—NEW DEAL

output and prices under collective capitalist control. Restrictive planning took a great leap forward under the New Deal, and was largely effective in preventing the increase in farm prices brought about by the Administration's other manœuvres from greatly increasing the farmer's real purchasing power.

The question that concerns us is how far the pre-crisis situation has really been changed, either temporarily or for good and all, since the advent of President Roosevelt. It is extraordinarily difficult, above all for anyone who is not resident in the United States, and is compelled to take his evidence for the most part from printed records rather than from daily contact with those concerned, to disentangle the essential from the inessential, or even to appreciate what has really happened up to the present time in the course of what is variously called either the 'Roosevelt experiment' or the 'New Deal.' Nevertheless some attempt at this must clearly be made. For President Roosevelt's strivings towards reconstruction and revival are as surely the outstanding example of an attempt at a sort of reformed Capitalism as the Russian Five-Year Plans are of Socialist planning in the world of to-day. Italy under Fascism, and Germany, first under Brüning and subsequently under the Nazis, have also made large-scale experiments in the planning of capitalist industry, and something has been said in the previous chapter about what has happened in these countries. But both the scale of the American experiment and the fact that it has taken place in what has been in recent times the greatest and richest capitalist country in the world plainly mark it out for pride of place in any study of the prospects and possibilities of capitalist reformation.

Moreover, whereas in both Germany and Italy the development of a partly planned economic system has gone on to the accompaniment of a political revolution, which has totally destroyed both the institutions of parliamentary control and the organised working-class movement as a counterpoise to the capitalist forces, in the United States the wide powers conferred upon the President for dealing with the emergency have not so far involved any outward change of political system. The President has got his emergency powers from Congress; and most of them have been voted to him only for a very limited period. Congress is still free to vote down or to override the President, if it so wishes or dares, upon a wide range of issues; and if it has done this but seldom, the explanation is to be found not in the existence of any sort of 'dictatorship,' or 'one-party State,' as in Italy or Germany, but rather in the immense known backing of the President among the great majority of the population, and in the absence of any alternative to his authority. Congress has been well aware that the population of the United States has looked to the President far more than to its members to find an issue out of the all too pervasive and oppressive troubles which have afflicted the people, and Congress has known too well what the temper of the people has been to venture to stand decisively in the President's way as long as he has retained his hold upon popular confidence. Moreover, the New Deal, so far from destroying or weakening the American working-class movement, such as it is, has at the very least done a little to strengthen it, and to increase its bargaining power. As far as democracy is possible in a capitalist society based on wide inequalities of status and income, the authority of President Roosevelt has been a democratic authority, and his experiment in capitalist reform an experiment made under the institutions of capitalist democracy.

President Roosevelt's real difficulties have lain so far, not with Congress, but with the American Constitution and its interpreter, the Supreme Court of the United States. At an early stage, all the codemaking provisions of the N.R.A. were disallowed by the Supreme Court, which also passed adverse judgment on the Frasier-Lemke Farm Indebtedness Act and several other important parts of the New Deal, and may at any time pronounce decisively against some other of the President's major measures. A written Federal Constitution, and above all one drawn up in the 'age of liberty' and carefully made difficult to amend, obviously puts enormous obstacles in the way of any sort of effective planning, even of a purely capitalist kind. It is still more plainly inconsistent with any sort of Socialist planning, which would at once come up against not only 'State rights,' but also the entire conception of the 'rights of property' embodied in the Constitution. The wonder is that, in face of the Constitution and the Supreme Court, it has been possible for President Roosevelt to go as far as he has actually gone. Clearly he could not have gone much further without getting the Constitution amended; and that is probably beyond both his power and his desires, to the extent to which it would be necessary in order to endow him with real authority to plan American industry. I do not venture, however, in this matter to put on the prophet's mantle. It is enough for my present point to observe that the New Deal, without upsetting democratic principles, has gone far enough to make very difficult a reversion to pure individualism, and has unloosed forces which may in the end revise the Constitution, if not constitutionally, at any rate in an unconstitutionally democratic way.

This gives it a special importance. For if President Roosevelt's New Deal were to succeed in restoring to health, according to capitalist standards of well-being, the debilitated economic system of the

AMERICAN 'PLANNING'—NEW DEAL

United States, he would have demonstrated to the world not only that Capitalism can, by the right adjustments, be given a new lease of life, but also that this can be done without a political revolution of so drastic a character as to suppress and dissipate the forces antagonistic to Capitalism. It can no doubt be argued that the known weakness of Socialism in the United States, and its failure to secure so far the backing of the organised working-class movement, make possible in America what would be quite impossible in countries where Socialism has struck deeper roots. This may be true, but the point remains that the durable success of the Roosevelt experiment would demonstrate conclusively that economic recovery under Capitalism is reconcilable with the retention of such freedoms of speech and organisation and private living as the capitalist system has hitherto usually been prepared to recognise as the necessary accompaniments to its advance.

In saying this, I have been assuming that the New Deal in its essential features is properly to be regarded as an experiment in some sort of capitalist planning. Of its capitalist character there can, of course, be no doubt. For every attempt has been made at each stage to operate it to the fullest possible extent by calling upon the capitalists to devise and work the appropriate organisations for its conduct. The countless Government agencies that have been set up have for their object not to take the management of industry or agriculture, or even finance, out of the hands of the private capitalists and farmers and property-owners who have controlled them hitherto, but to rehabilitate these persons and the institutions of which they are in command in such a way as to enable them to resume their operations with success. This is most obviously true in the case of the National Recovery Act, which was designed to be worked through Code Authorities almost exclusively representing the industrialists themselves, with occasional representatives of labour, of the consumers, and even of the Administration, playing only a very minor part. But it is no less true of the reorganisation of banking after the crisis of 1933. For the President, so far from advancing towards any further socialisation of the American banking system, beyond what is already embodied in the Federal Reserve Acts, devoted his energies on the morrow of the crisis mainly to the use of public funds in order to enable closed banks to be reopened, and used these funds in such a way as to enable the banks to escape as soon as possible from the temporary controls which the emergency had compelled him to impose. Nor is it less true in the case of agriculture. For there the main efforts have been directed to so reducing the burden of farm indebtedness and so far raising the effective levels of farm prices as to make it possible for the American farmer again to

AMERICAN 'PLANNING'—NEW DEAL

get for himself a tolerable living in very much the old way.

In fact, President Roosevelt's main endeavour, from the moment when he first assumed office up to the present time, has been to restore the profitability of American private enterprise over the widest possible field. Under the institutions of Capitalism the level of production and the numbers employed depend essentially on the extent of the area over which the possessors and controllers of productive resources can see a tolerable prospect of being able to use these resources so as to realise a profit. If President Roosevelt wanted to get people back to work under the institutions of Capitalism, there was only one way in which he could set about it. He had somehow or other to make it profitable for capitalist employers to employ a larger number of persons in producing an increased quantity of goods. There was no choice at all about this, for there is and can be no other way under Capitalism of getting people back to work. Public works may be used temporarily as a means of expanding the volume of employment. But their object, under Capitalism, is essentially to bring the capitalist employer back into action by improving the level of effective demand. If they pass beyond this, and the attempt is made to use them as permanent agencies for maintaining the demand for labour, difficulties inevitably accumulate. For either public debts continue to pile up till they become unbearable, or recourse must be had to monetary inflation, which becomes cumulative until the entire economy is brought to a stand.

It is, of course, perfectly true that President Roosevelt's ambitions were not confined to the mere getting of people back into employment by offering the capitalist a higher inducement to employ them. He did undoubtedly think in terms of reform as well as recovery, and he was compelled so to think because of the discredit into which the institutions of American Capitalism had fallen by reason of the crisis and the plain inability of big business leaders and of the Hoover Administration to discover any remedy for it. The President had to satisfy those who had placed him in office that he was endeavouring to reform the system, as well as to set the wheels turning again. But unless he was prepared totally to alter the basis of American economic life he had no alternative to putting recovery in practice a long way before reform. For reforms were bound to a substantial extent, at least in the first instance, to limit rather than to extend the area of profitability for capitalist enterprise; and it was therefore impossible for the President to push on more than a little way with reforms in the capitalist system until he had succeeded in so stimulating recovery that the burdens of reform could be successfully sustained by the

AMERICAN 'PLANNING'—NEW DEAL 153

capitalists without provoking a recession. Moreover, if he did succeed in bringing about recovery on such a scale, it was highly probable that the pressure from public opinion for the reform of Capitalism would promptly die a natural death.

I am not concerned at this point either to praise or to criticise the New Deal on account of these characteristics, but only to bring out its essential nature. President Roosevelt has been trying not to establish a new economic system in the United States, but to make the old system work again by drastic overhauling and repair. We can discuss later whether this was the right or the wrong thing to attempt. The point for the present is that there can be no doubt at all that this is what President Roosevelt has been attempting from first to last.

Of course it would have been impossible to attempt the rehabilitation of American Capitalism without substantially changing it in the process. Even if the New Deal were in course of time totally to disappear, the marks of its passage upon the structure of American economic life would certainly be in many respects permanent. To take one example, even if the anti-trust laws were allowed to come back into full operation and even though the N.R.A. Codes have expired altogether, it is nevertheless quite impossible to undo the effects of the closer co-operative relationships which have been established during the emergency between American business men in the same branch of production, or for the courts to administer the anti-trust laws in quite the same manner or spirit as before. That, however, does not alter the fact that the N.R.A. Codes were themselves so devised and administered as to modify as little as possible the structure and working of either individual capitalist businesses or existing trade associations—so that they could easily be withdrawn in such a way as to leave the outward structure of the American business world very little different from what it was before they were introduced. Apart from the changed relationship between one business and another, which could not be wholly undone, the entire elaborate system of Codes and Administrators and Boards under the N.R.A. could disappear at a wave of the Judges' wand, and in its fading all the insubstantial pageant could dissolve and leave not a wrack behind. To some extent, Big Business has undoubtedly been strengthened at the expense of the smaller employers; but this has only speeded up a process that was going on quite apart from the N.R.A.

Or again, the banks, having repaid their debts to the Reconstruction Finance Corporation and been allowed to transfer the preferred stock now held on Government account back into private hands—which they have largely been enabled to do as a result of the effectiveness of the President's policy in increasing the value of their securities—

can regain full liberty of action, subject only to such controls as the Federal Reserve System already imposed on most of them, or at any rate on most of the big ones, before the crash of 1933. The President can renounce or lose his special powers over the open market policy of the Federal Reserve Banks and over the Federal Reserve Board. Banking can become again fully as much a private capitalist affair as it was before the crisis, though probably, in the interests of sound capitalist banking, the prohibition of the linking of deposit banks with 'security affiliates' will be maintained. More banks than before have been brought under the discipline of the Federal Reserve System, and certain other restrictions imposed on the actions of bankers as a result of the crisis have become a recognised part of capitalist banking practice. The United States can return to the international gold standard at whatever parity may seem most suitable at the time of the return, or can even adopt some sort of permanent 'managed' currency system, to be operated without political interference by the banking institutions. The President's power to manipulate the mechanism of currency and credit can be simply withdrawn, leaving the American financial machine not very much different from what it was intended to be when the Federal Reserve System was first instituted after the crisis of 1907. Certain holes in the Federal Reserve Act of 1913 have been patched or mended, but otherwise the banking system has already, now the crisis is largely over, reverted to the *status quo ante*.

Or take the case of agriculture. The Roosevelt policy, as far as it relates to the refinancing of farm mortgages and the provision of agricultural credit, was clearly designed to re-establish the farm *entrepreneur* upon his holding in such a way as to enable him to carry on production for profit much as before. As far as it related to the restoration of agricultural prices to a more remunerative level and to the re-establishment of the 'farmer's ratio' between agricultural and other prices, it aimed only at achieving a result which, once secured, would remove the necessity for further intervention by the Administration, if, as was hoped, the new equilibrium of prices, once established, proved to be self-sustaining.

It is true that, as far as the agricultural policy involved the public purchase of farm produce in order to avoid glutting the market, the reduction of the areas under certain crops, and the positive withdrawal of certain lands from cultivation, the New Deal was employing methods which could not be so easily abandoned in favour of the practices which it replaced. But it is significant that those measures, which are likely to be the hardest parts of the New Deal to liquidate, are precisely those whose purely temporary character has been most

AMERICAN 'PLANNING'—NEW DEAL

strongly emphasised by the Administration itself. They were forced upon the President by the exceptional severity of the crisis in the agricultural districts, not deliberately adopted in pursuance of any clearly conceived plan of economic reorganisation.

It is indeed in the field of agricultural policy that the Roosevelt experiment has been most obviously lacking in consistency and clearness of objective. For the future of American agriculture is inseparably bound up with the future place of the United States in the world economic system. As the Secretary of Agriculture, Mr. Wallace, has repeatedly pointed out, America has to choose between a low tariff policy which will admit enough imports to enable foreigners to pay for a large volume of agricultural exports from the United States, and a policy of industrial self-sufficiency in respect of manufactured goods and most raw materials, which carries with it a necessary curtailment in the volume of American exports. If the second of these policies was preferred, or even if a nearer approach was made to it than to its opposite, as has been in fact the case, there could be no alternative to a drastic curtailment of the acreage devoted to cotton, wheat, tobacco, and certain other primary crops, or to a limitation of the output of hogs and cattle. Indeed, even if American tariff policy were to become as liberal as it seems at all possible to think that it could become in the near future, the need for a curtailment of output in many forms of agriculture would almost certainly remain, though it would of course need to be pushed less far than under a régime of high tariffs. For, as productivity increases and the standard of living rises in the less developed countries, a smaller proportion of total income goes to the purchase of primary foodstuffs. Moreover, the downward tendency of birth rates in the chief importing countries seems certain, even apart from changes in their own policy in respect of admitting imports, to cut down the external demand for the primary products of the United States. The cotton industry will be carried on more largely in the Far East and with Far Eastern cotton, whatever tariff policy the American Government may pursue. A régime of freer trade would diminish the need for readjustment of the American agricultural system, but it could not possibly go so far as to make readjustment unnecessary.

Under the New Deal, the policy pursued was that of restricting agricultural output in order to raise the level of farm prices; and to some extent this policy undoubtedly succeeded in narrowing the margin between the prices at which farmers had to buy and sell. But most of the measures of restriction, except the acquisition of 'sub-marginal' land for public purposes, which has not been on a very extensive scale, have been conceived of as temporary. Even so, they stand in sharp contrast to the expansionist tendencies of the rest of the Roosevelt programme, and there can be no doubt that the President contemplated with deep dislike the prospect of having permanently to reduce the scale of American farming enterprise—the more so because the very rapid advance in agricultural productivity, which has already brought about a big contraction in the numbers occupied in land work, aggravates the social consequences of restriction. In face of this difficulty, the Administration was undoubtedly eager to do anything it could to increase the volume of American agricultural exports —provided this could be done without lowering dollar prices to the American farmer. The powers conferred on the President drastically to reduce tariff duties, even without the consent of the Senate, clearly contemplated the negotiation of agreements designed to secure a market abroad for a larger volume of farm produce, even at the cost of lessening the protection accorded to American industries. This power, however, has not been greatly used as yet, and it would be very difficult for the President to use it extensively at a time when it might, by lessening the area or profitability for American industrialists, stand seriously in the way of the recovery part of his programme. In effect, the future policy of the United States in respect of economic nationalism and internationalism is still undetermined. But until this is determined it will be quite impossible to arrive at any long-run policy for American agriculture.

Evidently a great deal hangs on this decision. If it goes mainly in favour of economic nationalism, it may be possible again to restrict Government intervention in industry to the manipulation of the tariff, but it will assuredly not be possible to leave American agriculture to adjust itself to the consequences of such a policy under the attrition of purely economic forces. No President, however powerful, dare leave the farmers at the mercy of the economic blizzard which such a decision would necessarily unloose upon them. But on the other hand, dare any President face the hostility from big business interests, and probably from the industrial workers as well, which the alternative of a low tariff policy would involve? No President dare take such a course until recovery is well enough secured to ensure profitability over a wide field, even in face of tariff reductions. But, if recovery did seem to have reached such a point, how much power to do anything would be left in the President's hands? On this issue, as on many others, President Roosevelt, almost as much as a far weaker President, has been compelled to compromise. But even a compromise which involves some degree of continued assistance to agriculture is bound to make it difficult for the Administration to withdraw from intervention nearly as rapidly in the agricultural as it could in the industrial and financial fields.

Of course, in all these fields withdrawal is conditional upon either success, at least up to a certain point, or dramatic failure. Most of the steps that were taken under the New Deal were of such a nature that they could not be gone back upon unless they led either to a complete collapse of the New Deal as a whole, or to such a restoration of capitalist profitability as would give business men over a wide field confidence in their ability to carry on without further Government help. President Roosevelt created among the American people a state of mind which compelled him to go on making fresh experiments until he either succeeded or decisively failed. There were, of course, at all times plenty of business men who urged that experimentation had gone quite far enough, that, the worst of the crisis being apparently over, business could best be left to make its own gradual recovery by itself, and that the measures of Government intervention had best be as rapidly as possible withdrawn before the structure of private enterprise was unduly impaired. But, whatever business men might say, a policy of this sort was politically impracticable as long as many millions of workers remained unemployed and in need of relief, and a large proportion of the farm population was still

F

making ends meet only with the aid of Government largesse. Fanatical advocates of private enterprise might clamour, and might even score here and there a secondary success. For the President knows well how to *reculer* as well as *sauter*. But the reception of the Supreme Court's decision against the N.R.A. Codes was highly significant. Many of those business men who had been clamouring most loudly for 'freedom' when they did not expect to get it stood aghast when the Supreme Court handed it to them. As long as the conditions of widespread unemployment and impoverishment remained, the New Deal was bound to go on—unless it crashed. It could not, save in secondary matters, go back, or even stand still.

What has been said so far therefore amounts to saying that, if the New Deal succeeded, it would in essentials only re-establish American Capitalism in its old forms, and was not designed to do anything towards the institution of a different economic system. We shall have to come back at a later stage to consider the consequences which are likely to follow the success which it has achieved in re-establishing the profitability of capitalist enterprise. But what if it had failed, or, in the effort to avert failure, been driven on, despite the difficulties which the Constitution put in its way, towards far more drastic forms of interference with private enterprise? If it had failed and crashed, as private

AMERICAN 'PLANNING'—NEW DEAL 163

enterprise crashed in 1929 and still more in 1933, there would have been an open field—a field so open that it is useless to attempt to spot the possible winner. If, however, the President had been driven on to more radical forms of intervention, it seems clear that these would for the most part have merely continued and expanded the existing policy of trying to stimulate capitalist recovery, and would not have taken shape in an endeavour to build up an alternative economic system. President Roosevelt himself declared emphatically that no one in his senses would attempt in America to supersede the profit motive; and that means that, if his measures had failed, he would have tried the effect of intensifying them rather than have turned to anything of a radically different sort. He would have created yet more money by extensive open-market operations, made possible by Government borrowing, would have instituted yet more public works and disbursed yet more relief, in the hope that these two methods would be jointly effective in expanding consumers' demand. He would have continued to manipulate the currency by further exchange operations, purchases of gold and silver, and perhaps even by further devaluation or depreciation of the dollar. Possibly he would have resumed his attempts to reduce hours and raise wages under the Wagner Labour Bill or in other ways, after the N.R.A. had failed him, though in this field he appears to have realised that the consequent addition to costs was calculated rather to limit than to extend the area of capitalist profitability. Probably he would have pressed on with further measures of industrial and social legislation on the lines of his existing schemes of social insurance. What he would not have done, as far as it is possible to judge from the spirit of his public utterances, was even to contemplate any fundamental change in the structure of the American business system. President Roosevelt is no Socialist, but a capitalist reformer; and the New Deal was not designedly a move towards any sort even of semi-Socialism but rather an attempt to set American Capitalism once more firmly on a profit-making basis.

We can, then, safely treat the New Deal as an attempt to re-establish private capitalist enterprise. Regarded in this light, what does it amount to? It clearly falls very far short of any attempt, even temporarily, to plan the output of the American economic system so as to meet the needs of the consuming public, or to plan the distribution of incomes so as to bring them into balance with the available productive power, or to achieve by collective effort a full and balanced use of the available resources. Except in the case of oil and of certain agricultural commodities, hitherto largely produced for export, there has been no attempt to regulate the volume of production of any particular commodity, save to the extent to which this was done voluntarily for a time by the Code Authorities under the N.R.A. in certain industries in pursuit of their own sectional capitalist advantage. The American *entrepreneur* continued in most cases, under the New Deal as before, to produce what he liked in what quantities he regarded as most likely to yield him a profit. There was nothing in the nature of a plan in the sense in which the Russians plan their output. There was, indeed, some attempt to raise wage-incomes both by expanding total employment, through the reduction of hours and through public works, and by securing the observance of minimum hourly and weekly wage-rates under the various industrial Codes. But the attempt to reduce hours and to raise wages, after the initial drive during the period of extreme capitalist disorganisation, was more and more half-heartedly pursued in face of capitalist opposition and of a growing sense in the President's own mind of its inconsistency with capitalist revival. The provisions of the Industrial Recovery Act for the general recognition of the right of collective bargaining were never effectively enforced in a number of the leading industries, though without them the endeavour to increase wages was certain to fail in view of the weakness of Labour Unionism over the greater part of industry. For the most part the wage increases that were enforced were no more than the corollary to the higher price policy which was being simultaneously pursued. Their effect was rather to preserve the purchasing power of the wage-earners in employment in face of rising prices than to increase the share of the wage-earners in the total national income. In so far as this has been increased at all, the increase has been due far more to the outpouring of public money through public works and relief schemes than to the raising of wages under the New Deal.

A good deal more was done by direct loans and subsidies and by other measures designed to raise farm prices to increase the income of the agricultural part of the community. These measures, however, were designed rather to remove the quite abnormal relative depression of farmers' purchasing power, still thought of as due in the main to exceptional and temporary causes, than to alter permanently by public intervention the operation of the 'economic laws' which affect the distribution of the national income. The Roosevelt policy aimed at readjusting price ratios which were regarded as having somehow got out temporarily of an adjustment which was supposed to be 'right' and 'natural.' But that done, it seems as if reliance was still placed on the principle of 'marginal productivity' to deal out economic justice to the various claimants to shares in the national output

AMERICAN 'PLANNING'—NEW DEAL

of goods and services. President Roosevelt may indeed still discover that the ratios between farm and other prices which he regards as 'natural' no longer correspond to the laws of marginal productivity in face of the changed relative conditions of supply and demand in agriculture and in industry. But the point is, not that the ratios which an attempt has been made to establish are likely in fact to be self-sustaining, but that the policy of readjustment was based on the belief that the existing ratios were somehow abnormal and unnatural. This belief may have been right or wrong, but it was undoubtedly the basis of the policy which was followed.

In industry what the New Deal had accomplished before the Supreme Court upset the N.R.A. was broadly to equip each branch of production with a 'Code of Fair Competition' administered by a Code Authority of the *entrepreneurs*' own choosing, subject to the proviso that the decisions of the Code Authorities should be liable to veto by the Administration. The Code Authorities had in fact very wide powers. They were entitled to fix minimum prices and to prohibit sales at less than these prices. They were authorised to restrict output or the installation of new plant or the use of existing plant. They were empowered to impose uniform systems of costing and to prohibit sales at less than 'cost price,' whatever that highly ambiguous phrase might be considered to mean. They were able to compel firms to make declarations, open to the whole industry, of their prices and conditions of sale. Moreover, a substantial majority in a trade was authorised in all these respects to coerce a reluctant minority, subject to the Administration's endorsement of its proposals; and, if a trade refused to draw up a Code for itself, the Administration had full authority to impose a Code upon it, even against its will.

The veto reserved to the Administration seemed at first sight to afford to the consumer a large protection against the abuse of these powers; but in fact the protection was very much less than would appear. For the entire public organisation of the N.R.A. had to be improvised at extraordinarily short notice, in a country which possesses no Civil Service or administrative equipment at all comparable with that of Great Britain. The N.R.A. Administration was a mushroom growth; and as it was called upon to deal almost simultaneously with the drafting and working of literally hundreds of separate Codes for different industries and trades, it was utterly impossible for it to give more than a most cursory supervision to the measures taken by the industrialists under the powers accorded them. In practice, the N.R.A. meant that, subject to a few very broad and general prohibitions and requirements, the Code Authority in each industry was able to do pretty much what it liked, with hardly any interference by the Administration and hardly any effective representation of the consumers' interests.

All these extensive powers were, however, permissive and not mandatory, and in fact most industries did not make any great use of the majority of them. The number of schemes involving definite restriction of output was never very great, nor were these schemes carried nearly so far as similar arrangements in other countries have gone, even without any special intervention or encouragement on the part of the Government. The effects of uniform costing and mutual disclosure of prices and conditions of sale were more far-reaching, and a good deal was done to check for the time being some of the grosser forms of corrupt and unfair competition hitherto prevalent in many industries. But these developments only carried further tendencies which already existed in American business, and were already being fostered by Government action, even in face of the anti-trust laws, before the depression set in. They did not change the character of the American industrial system in any of its essential features.

Much use was indeed made in certain industries, notably those producing the more standardised types of commodity, of the price-fixing powers accorded under the N.R.A. The Codes undoubtedly did a great deal not only to eliminate what is called 'weak selling,' but actually to raise prices by common agreement among the members of a trade. But these provisions of the N.R.A. led to so much public outcry that, in face of the long-established public hostility to compulsory price maintenance under the orders of what are in effect capitalist combines, the price-fixing powers conceded under the N.R.A. had already been modified even before the Supreme Court's decision swept the whole experiment in publicly authorised price-regulation away. Doubtless, even though these powers have disappeared, they have left behind them a legacy of closer common action in respect of prices than has prevailed hitherto over the greater part of American business. But price-fixing soon ceased to receive any official support from the Administration, and quite definitely it has come again under the ban of the law.

The provisions of the N.R.A. Codes which fixed minimum wage-rates and maximum hours of employment and limited or prohibited altogether child labour are of more fundamental importance. When the N.R.A. was launched, its principal objects were declared to be an expansion both of the number of employed workers and of the real incomes of those employed. The minimum wage-rates fixed in the Codes for the various industries, together with the additional provisions which most of them contained

AMERICAN 'PLANNING'—NEW DEAL 171

for some increase in the remuneration of the higher paid classes of labour, did at the outset contribute substantially to an advance in working-class purchasing power, and the same effect was achieved for industries which remained for some time outside the Codes by the general 'Blanket Code' introduced by the President on a voluntary basis. But, as we have seen, a good deal of this advantage to the workers was speedily wiped out by the rise in prices which accompanied the introduction of the Codes, and still more was subsequently cancelled by the effects of currency depreciation. The Codes did doubtless achieve a nearer approach to standardisation of wage-rates than existed before their introduction, and did thus limit competitive wage-cutting under the influence of the depression. But they did not go much beyond this save for the very lowest paid workers; and after the first impetus the President appears, in deference to capitalist hostility to the further raising of costs, to have modified the view which he expressed at the outset that employers could afford to pay much higher wages, provided only that all competing firms were made subject to the same obligations in this respect. Labour at any rate got much less out of the N.R.A. than it was promised and had every reason to expect; and the Labour Unions did not, in most industries, prove nearly strong enough to exact by industrial pressure what the President was showing less and less disposition to enforce upon the strongly resistant capitalist class.

It has indeed to be recognized that the Codes as a whole were never effectively enforced. Unsure of the constitutional position, and unwilling in any case to provoke a general conflict with the forces of big business at a time when recovery seemed to him much more important than reform, the President and his subordinate administrators very seldom advanced beyond persuasion in their endeavours to secure observance of the provisions of the Codes. Employers who flouted the Codes in this or that particular respect were often argued with endlessly, both by their fellow-employers and by the countless 'compliance' officers and committees of the N.R.A. Administration. But they were not, save in the rarest instances, actually coerced by an ultimate appeal to the law. Nor did the zeal to secure compliance by moral pressure show itself equally strong in all industries or in respect of all the provisions of the N.R.A. and of the Codes.

In particular, as we have seen, the clause in the National Recovery Act itself which purported to secure to all workers the right of collective bargaining through Labour Unions of their own choosing, and immunity from any coercion to join 'Company Unions' created and controlled by their employers, remained a dead letter in a number of the major industries. The steel and automobile industries for the most part successfully ignored it, and so did large sections of the coal industry and of many others. In the early stages of the N.R.A. it seemed for a time as if Labour Unionism in the United States might at last come into its own, and with the aid of the Administration succeed in breaking down the 'Company Union' mechanism devised by the employers and in building up an effective organisation of its own in all the major industries. But fear of Socialist 'extremism' among the leaders of the American Federation of Labour conspired with the President's reluctance to face a battle with big business to defeat these hopes. Labour Unionism soon grew in total numerical strength, but as an effective bargaining force it spread only a little way beyond the limited group of industries in which it was already an important power before the crisis began. Even in August, 1934, the American Federation of Labour had less than three million paid-up members, whereas the number organised in 'Company Unions' was said to be as high as ten millions. It is true that, apart from the paid-up membership of the American Federation of Labour, there was a very large body of workers who had only dropped out of the Unions on account of unemployment. The A.F. of L. claimed to represent almost twice as many members as were actually paying dues. But, even if this claim is to be accepted, the combined strength of the A.F. of L.

and of the Labour Unions not affiliated to it can hardly have been more than six millions, or about one-fifth of the wage and salary workers eligible to belong to it. The A.F. of L. increased its paid-up membership by nearly 700,000 soon after the N.R.A. came in; but it had still an enormous way to travel before it could claim to be representative of the American working class in at all the same sense as the Trades Union Congress can claim to represent the workers in Great Britain. Moreover, the company unions went on growing very much faster than the Unions affiliated to the A.F. of L.; for the most marked effect of the 'collective bargaining' clauses of the N.R.A. was to stimulate the employers' zeal to protect themselves from such unionism by organising bodies of this type.

In the absence of effective working-class organisation save in a few industries, the wage-fixing provisions of the N.R.A. were bound to be of small effect over the greater part of the industrial field. As prices rose, the minimum wages laid down in the Codes became less important. But wages could hardly be raised further, in face of strong capitalist opposition, and might at any time be drastically reduced, unless there were powerful Labour Unions to press for their maintenance. Moreover, such pressure as the Administration was prepared to apply was for the most part confined to the basic minima for the lowest paid grades of workers, and did little or nothing for those who were in receipt of more than the lowest rates. These latter therefore depended for what they got on the bargaining power of the Labour Unions; and where this was lacking there was even some danger that increases in the minimum rates might be offset by worsening of wages and conditions among the higher grades. If the President had seriously desired to increase the workers' share of the national income more than it could be increased merely by adding to the numbers employed, he could have been sure of doing this only if he had been prepared to help the workers to create effective organisations for the furtherance of their interests—that is, to compel the employers to give real effect to the collective bargaining provisions of the Wagner Act. But to do this would have plunged him at once into a struggle with big business, on which he relied as the chief agent of national recovery; and ranged on his own side he would have found only two considerable forces—the narrow-minded egotistical monopolistic anti-Bolshevik-complex-ridden American Federation of Labour, and a socialistically or even communistically minded left wing with which he was determined to have no truck for fear of alienating 'moderate' sympathies.

Nevertheless, new forces were stirring in the minds of the American workers. Slow as was the growth of the American Federation of Labour, the desire for collective action was rapidly gaining ground, and was being held in check only by the blank refusal to recognise Trade Unionism in many of the major industries. When at length, Mr. John L. Lewis, at the head of the United Mine Workers, broke away from the traditionalism of the old craft union movement, and founded the Committee for Industrial Organisation in the teeth of the American Federation of Labour's bitter hostility, progressive working-class sentiment rallied round the new movement. Nothing much happened until Mr. Roosevelt's sensational victory over Governor Landon, in which he received the full support of the Lewis movement. But thereafter the Committee for Industrial Organisation felt strong enough to act; and within a few months it wrested recognition from the General Motors Corporation by means of a great strike, in which 'stay-in' methods were employed, and induced the powerful Steel Corporation to accept collective bargaining without a stoppage of work. These events opened a new chapter in American Labour history; but they belong to a period subsequent to that of the New Deal. They arose out of President Roosevelt's measures, and his victory in the presidential election; but they were not of his doing.

For, it must never be forgotten, President Roosevelt believes in the profit-making system. In his own words, amplifying President Cleveland's dictum to suit the changed conditions of the twentieth century, he wants private as well as public office to be regarded as a public trust. He wants the business man, without ceasing to have regard to his own private interest, to regard also the interest of the public as a whole. He believes implicitly that it is possible to get rich to the glory of God—to pursue the public interest and private self-interest at one and the same time without the two needing to clash. That belief lies at the root of his policy, and if that goes he has nothing left to light his course. He does indeed believe that private self-interest needs to be guided and controlled in order to help it to serve public ends; and to that extent he has moved far from the old let-alone optimism of the nineteenth century. But he does still believe that profit, the desire for personal gain, is and must be for most men an essential stimulus to make them give of their best, and that the Socialist dream of a world without profit is and must be no more than a dream. In that opinion probably most Americans still think him right; and as long as they do think him right he *is* right in holding that there can be no alternative basis for the American economic system. But it is another question whether he is right in believing that American Capitalism can be successfully reconstructed on its present basis, or on the basis of any reconciliation between private profit and public interest that he will be able to devise. It is, however, assuredly true that neither in the United States nor anywhere else can there be any alternative to Capitalism, except chaos, until at least a large number of people in the community can be induced to believe in the possibility of enterprise based on public service and not on the profit motive.

It is not easy to believe this, perhaps above all in the United States, where the 'almighty dollar' has been so exalted, and the prestige of public service been for the most part so low. But unless it is believed, no real alternative to an attempt at capitalist reconstruction exists. It is probable that in the United States there was, when the crisis had to be faced, no practicable alternative to President Roosevelt's attempt to set the capitalist system back on its feet, though this situation might have changed very rapidly if his attempt had failed. It might change very rapidly in the future if its temporary success in restoring business activity proved to be merely the prelude to a new crisis.

Among the host of measures which make up the New Deal, let us try to isolate those which are essential from the standpoint of their relationship to a planned economic system. Broadly, these essential measures fall under six heads—those dealing respectively with money and banking, with capital issues and stock market speculation, with industrial

AMERICAN 'PLANNING'—NEW DEAL 179

production and prices, with labour conditions and wage incomes, with agricultural production and farm conditions, and, finally, with public works and provision for the unemployed.

Something must be said at the outset about the general character of the American banking system. The Federal Reserve Act of 1913 was designed to introduce an element of planning in order to end the chaos which the crisis of 1907 had revealed. Under that Act the country was equipped with a network of Central Banks, partly Government-controlled and all co-ordinated under the authority of a governing agency, the Federal Reserve Board. The new Federal Reserve Banks were designed not primarily as profit-making institutions—though they were intended to pay reasonable dividends on their capital—but as bankers' banks, to supply the ordinary commercial banks with credit facilities, especially for the rediscounting of eligible short-term bills and other tokens of indebtedness. They were intended further to bring about a better utilisation of the available bank reserves and to make easier the movement of funds from one part of the country to another. The idea was that the division of the whole area of the United States into twelve Federal Reserve Districts, each with its own bank, would help to remedy the previous tendency for funds to be drawn away from all other areas to New York. All banks operating under Federal law were compelled to join the Federal Reserve System, and banks under State law were allowed to become members on complying with the conditions of membership. But the commercial banks, whether they became members or not, remained purely private institutions, free to follow whatever policy they chose, subject to the restrictions as to minimum reserves placed upon them by statute. Moreover, the Federal Reserve Banks, though Government-created, were placed under Boards of Direction chosen chiefly not by the Government but by the member banks as representative of banking and business interests within their respective areas. The Federal Reserve Board, itself a Government agency, did indeed appoint a minority of the Directors to each Federal Reserve Bank, and this minority included the Chairman, who also acted as Federal Reserve Agent for the district. But, under this system, the main control rested with the commercial bankers, and there was no attempt till after the crisis of 1933 to bring commercial banking policy under any sort of Government control, or even to plan the activities of the commercial banks in any way.

The Federal Reserve system did, however, embody an endeavour to lessen the chaos in American banking and to bring it in certain respects under some sort of central control. During the greater part of the post-war period there was under its auspices at least some attempt to plan the development of monetary conditions, as apart from the operations of commercial banking. Extensive experiments were made from time to time in the use of open market policy for regulating the supply of money and thereby operating on rates of interest and price levels, and this policy was deliberately employed for the purpose of checking what was regarded as undue expansion or of combating tendencies towards business depression. Purchases and sales of securities in the open market were used, as they had long been used by the Bank of England, but on a far larger scale, as means of regulating the resources at the disposal of the commercial banks. During the boom period which preceded the Wall Street crash of 1929, the Federal Reserve Authorities seem clearly to have been attempting to employ the method of monetary management in such a way as to keep the 'general level of prices' nearly stable; and after the crash persistent attempts were made from time to time, long before President Roosevelt came to office, to mitigate depression and if possible promote recovery by means of an expansionist monetary policy.

It is now common knowledge that the endeavour to stabilise the 'general level of prices' in face of rising productivity in both industry and agriculture and of world conditions that were steadily depressing the prices of American agricultural exports was one of the most serious factors aggravating disequilibrium during the boom. The more some prices fell, the more other prices had to be raised if the 'general level' was to remain the same; and the more money the banking system poured out in order to achieve price stability, the more irresistibly that money flowed out of the industrial and agricultural circulation into the financial circulation, where it was employed to skyrocket the prices of stocks and bonds and of real estate. As long as the boom lasted, there was no difficulty in getting additional credits taken up through the commercial banks, and to that extent the open market policy of the Federal Reserve System appeared to be a success. But the price of this success was disaster. For the infusion of the new money required to prevent the 'general level of prices' from falling aggravated the existing disequilibrium in the distribution of the community's current supply of purchasing power.

There can be no doubt that, during the period which preceded the Wall Street crash of 1929, the incomes accruing to the poorer sections of the community, including both farmers and the main body of wage-earners, lagged seriously behind the incomes accruing to the richer investing classes. It has been estimated that over the period from 1923 to 1929, the aggregate income derived from agriculture rose at an average annual rate of 2.7 per cent,

AMERICAN 'PLANNING'—NEW DEAL

whereas the aggregate income from manufacturing industry rose at a rate of 5.6 per cent. Moreover this latter increase was very unevenly divided between wage-earners and capitalists, their respective rates of increase being 3.1 and 7.3 per cent. In 1929, as compared with 1914, the aggregate income from agriculture had risen in purchasing power at wholesale prices by 21 per cent, whereas income from the extractive industries had risen by 107 per cent and income from manufactures by 134 per cent. In the last group labour's increase was 108 per cent of the 1914 purchasing power, and that of the capitalists 153 per cent. A measurement of industrial labour's aggregate purchasing power over a shorter period in terms of retail instead of wholesale prices yields an even less balanced result, showing an increase of only 6 per cent in the aggregate retail purchasing power of wages between 1923 and 1929.

Now, it has been estimated that the volume of physical output of goods of all sorts in the United States rose between 1922 and 1929 by 34 per cent, or between 1923 and 1929 (since 1922 was an abnormally low year) by 20 per cent. From 1922 to 1929 the average annual rate of increase has been put at 3.8 per cent, as against a population increase of 1.4 per cent. Production *per capita* was thus rising at an average annual rate of 2.4 per cent. Snyder's revised wage index for all classes of employees shows over the same period an average rise of about 20 per cent, or an annual rate of increase of 2.1 per cent. But for workers in manufacturing industry, according to the figures published by the National Industrial Conference Board, the total rise over these years was only 17 per cent, and the annual rate of increase 1.6 per cent. Moreover, in both these indices, by far the largest rise took place between 1922 and 1923, and 1923 is, as we have seen, a far more suitable base year. If 1923 instead of 1922 is taken as a starting point, the total rise in the Snyder index is only 9 per cent, and in the National Industrial Conference Board index only 6 per cent.

Now compare this position with that of the holders of common stocks in all types of corporate businesses. Between 1922 and 1929 the cash receipts of holders of common stocks increased by no less than 186 per cent, or between 1923 and 1929 by 158 per cent. It is true that this increase was not shared in by the bondholders, whose aggregate incomes remained at about the same level throughout the period. But this only made the position worse, because the common stocks are held largely by the richer members of the population. The position as between 1922 and 1929 can be stated most clearly by a comparison between certain types of income in terms of their estimated annual rates of increase.

AMERICAN INCOMES
Rates of Increase, 1922-1929

	Average Annual Rate of Increase Per Cent 1922-1929	Average Annual Rate of Increase Per Cent 1923-1929
All Wages (Snyder), Average Earnings	2.1	1.5
Industrial Wages (N.I.C.B.), Weekly Earnings	1.8	0.9
Aggregate Industrial Wages (Mills)	3.1	—
Farm Wages, Average Earnings	1.6	—
Aggregate Farm Incomes	2.7	—
Aggregate Net Corporation Incomes	7.3	—
Aggregate Corporation Dividends	12.8	—
Aggregate Receipts of Owners of Common Stocks	16.5	16.3
Physical Output of Goods	3.8	—

These figures yield abundant evidence of a gross maldistribution of the contemporary increase in the national income—the more so in that the discrepancy would in most cases be more glaring if the abnormal year 1922 had been excluded from the calculation.[1]

[1] For most of these figures see Mills, *Recent Economic Tendencies in the United States.*

Moreover, in every year between 1923 and 1928 the number of workers employed in manufacturing industries was well below the number employed in 1923, and even the boom of 1929 only carried the volume of employment just beyond the 1923 level. Thus, the apparent rate of increase of aggregate wage incomes between 1922 and 1929 is grossly misleading, for a large part of it is due to the inclusion of the bad year 1922.

In face of these conditions it was impossible for the American economic system not to get seriously out of balance. The enormous rise in the incomes accruing to the owners of stock market equities was obviously the direct consequence of applying a policy of price stabilisation under conditions of rapidly decreasing costs of production. For price stabilisation in these circumstances meant a swiftly widening margin between average costs and average selling prices, and thus opened up the prospect of abnormally high profits in all branches of production in which prices could be determined by internal as opposed to world forces. The disparity could doubtless have been corrected if, through the increase of wages, costs had risen as fast as efficiency improved, despite the decline in the quantity of labour needed for the production of a given quantity of goods. But it was out of the question for this to happen in face of the weakness of the American Labour movement and of the rapid displacement of labour by machinery which was the outstanding feature of the contemporary advance of productive technique. Unless the wage-earners had been very strongly organised, they could not possibly have maintained their position in face of the technological revolution that was going on. And in fact the patchiness of labour organisation, which was effective only in a limited group of trades, added fresh disparities to the distribution of the national income. Moreover, under the prevailing technical conditions, the successful forcing up of wage-rates would have intensified the displacement of labour by machinery, and so caused additional unemployment.

It is not of course the case, as some writers have suggested, that the enormous proportion of the national income which accrued to the rich owing to the widening margins between costs and selling prices led to a proportionate increase in the volume of investment as against consumption; for consumption was very greatly expanded during the period of the boom. The habit of stock market speculation spread during this period far beyond the rich, and many of the middle and upper working classes realised through speculation in securities capital profits which were very large in relation to the size of their normal incomes. These sections then proceeded to expand their standard of living by treating increments of capital as income, and the effect of this practice was to expand the current demand for consumers' goods. Investment did, of course, also expand very greatly, but not to anything like the extent to which it might have been expected to expand if the practice of speculation had not spread to a much larger section of the community.

To an appreciable extent the expansion of windfall 'incomes' from stock market speculation served to disguise and temporarily to offset the real disparity in the distribution of the national income from production, and the method of instalment purchase was a further instrument for preventing the current demand for consumers' goods from falling below the expanding supply at the stabilised level of prices. But these methods of temporarily expanding consumers' demand were essentially precarious, and the more reliance was placed upon them for preserving the balance between production and consumption, the more startling a crash was bound to follow as soon as anything disturbed the continuous flow of windfall profits. All through the first half of 1929 stock market prices were at a level which rested on the assumption of continuous and expanding prosperity. But at the same time the amount of money which the Federal Reserve System was compelled to pour out in order to keep the level of prices stable was mounting rapidly as more and more of the new money created for this purpose lapped over from the industrial into the financial circulation. Total bank loans rose from

$39\frac{1}{2}$ billion dollars in June, 1928, to well over 42 billions at the beginning of October, 1929, and over the same period total bank deposits rose by not far short of two billion dollars. It became evident, first, that the structure of prices would collapse unless the creation of new money continued at a rapidly increasing rate, and secondly that sooner or later a halt was bound to be called to a process of which the inflationary character was becoming more and more obvious. But as soon as these two facts came to be realised, even within a comparatively narrow circle of business people, a crash became inevitable. For producers were bound to begin slowing down production in the anticipation of a falling off of demand, and operators on the stock and produce and real estate markets were also bound to start selling in order to get out while the going was still good. This latter process however, once set to work, was bound to be cumulative in its effects. For as soon as a few people started selling, and prices in the stock, produce and real estate markets began to fall, there was certain to be a scramble to sell. This scramble was bound to be accentuated by the action of those who had made loans to speculators upon collateral security. For, as the value of securities fell, these creditors were certain to press either for repayment or for additional cover, thus compelling borrowers to throw securities on the market in order to pay off the loans which they had contracted. In view of the very widespread practice of speculating in large amounts of stock with a comparatively small cover, the dimensions to which this process of deflating inflated values could grow were almost unlimited.

Moreover, this scramble in turn was bound to react sharply and disastrously on the volume of purchasing power that would be currently expanded on consumers' as well as on producers' goods; for consumers' as well as producers' goods had been bought largely during the boom not out of real incomes but out of the paper profits of stock market and real estate speculation.

In the field of banking President Roosevelt, faced with a threatened paralysis of the entire financial structure at the very moment when he assumed office, devoted most of his efforts to restoring the financial 'soundness' of the banks. This he attempted in the first place by lending to them and investing in them through the Reconstruction Finance Corporation very large sums of money for the purpose of restoring their liquidity and enabling them to carry on current business. But it has been no part of his policy to acquire, in this or in any other way, any sort of permanent public ownership of the banking system. Indeed, his object has been to get rid as quickly as possible of the partial public ownership which was forced upon him by the crisis. Therefore, in the second place, he has followed a policy designed, by infusing additional supplies of money into the economic system, to raise the value of the banks' assets and increase the funds at their command so as to make it possible for them to repay the loans which they have received and to resume unfettered private ownership and control. He has, indeed, compelled the banks to discard their 'security affiliates,' which have been reconstructed as separate corporations. But this measure, intended to increase the soundness of commercial banking practice by ensuring greater liquidity and reducing bank speculation, only strengthens the banks as private capitalist institutions and is in no respect a move towards either increased State control or the institution of a planned economy.

It is indeed true that, by the new Banking Act passed by Congress in 1935, the President has strengthened the hold of the Federal Reserve Board over the supply of credit and the general policy of the banks and also bestowed upon the Administration an increased permanent control over the operations of the Board. But these measures go no further than to establish some degree of public control over monetary policy as distinct from commercial banking practice; and they leave the commercial banks fully as free from public interference as they are in other capitalist countries such as Great Britain and France. Moreover, it is quite possible that President Roosevelt's banking reforms will be substantially modified in their practical application. The commercial banks have no objection to an increased control over monetary policy by the Federal Reserve Board, but they want the Board itself to be constituted as an independent corporation wholly outside the range of Government intervention. If the President were to give way on this point, American capitalist banking would emerge from the crisis far more securely entrenched than ever before.

In the field of financial policy what 'planning' President Roosevelt has done has taken the form of monetary manipulation. The President has set out to 'plan' prices, first by open-market operations and Government spending designed to increase the quantity of money in circulation, and subsequently by following out a fantastic theory of the consequences of artificially depreciating the gold value of the dollar. The first of these policies, made effective by a great outpouring of money on public works and relief, subsidies to farmers, and the like, did undoubtedly raise prices in the home market. But it acted chiefly on the prices of industrial goods, which were already unduly high in relation to agricultural prices. The second policy was designed to help the agriculturists by increasing the dollar value of American exports without adding to their gold value, in the hope that this would react on the general level of agricultural prices in the country. In some degree it did have this effect. But for some

AMERICAN 'PLANNING'—NEW DEAL

time much of the benefit to the farmers was lost because of its results in depressing world prices, so that dollar prices rose much less than the gold value of the dollar fell. This policy therefore aggravated the world crisis without bringing any commensurate gain to the American farmers. What the farmers gained, which was considerable, was due mainly to the President's specific measures of agricultural relief and adjustment, and not to his monetary policy in bringing about an artificial depreciation of the dollar.

It cannot be too strongly emphasised that a planned monetary system is not, as the President's advisers often appeared to believe, an independent instrument of economic recovery, but only the necessary complement to a constructive economic policy. For recovery to be possible there must be enough money available to meet the needs of whatever economic policy it is decided to adopt, without increasing debt burdens or forcing an undue fall in prices as output is increased. Equally, there must not be so much money as to throw the economic system out of gear. But how much money there ought to be, and accordingly what levels of prices and costs, is a matter to be settled not independently but in accordance with the economic programme which the money is destined to finance. Monetary planning often seems to offer a convenient way of escape from the harder task of economic planning, but in fact it affords no escape. For an inappropriate monetary supply—by which I mean a supply unadjusted to current economic developments—can only distort the economic system and not assist towards any stable recovery.

We must therefore consider how far President Roosevelt in his 'crisis' legislation attempted to institute any sort of economic planning. In two instances he did at any rate set on foot constructive public experiments which might well form part of a national plan. These are the Tennessee Valley Authority and the Civilian Conservation Corps. Both these agencies are performing, directly under Federal auspices, development work which is calculated to improve the utilisation of American economic resources—the one by opening up a large backward region on the basis of an intensive use of electric power, and the other principally by conserving the vast forest resources of the country against destruction by fire. On a smaller scale are the schemes for improving land and preventing flood that have been carried through as part of the public works programme.

But when full allowance has been made for these drops in the ocean of public expenditure what is left? The planning of agricultural output? No doubt, in a sense, agricultural output has been 'planned'; but it has been 'planned' entirely for the purpose of decreasing output and throwing 'redundant' lands out of cultivation. Its object has been not the planning of output with a view to making fuller use of the available resources of production, but the raising of agricultural prices. I am not denying that there was a case for restricting the output of farm commodities which it was impossible to sell in the existing condition of the market, or even a case for remunerating farmers for the economic service of 'not raising hogs.' There may have been a case for both these things in the circumstances of the moment; but it is surely quite fantastic to regard curtailment of production as 'planning' unless it is accompanied by an effective transference of the displaced resources to more productive uses. The Agricultural Adjustment Administration has not been planning American agriculture: it has been engaged in rescue and relief work for the farmers on lines which were meant to avert the necessity for planning. Its purpose has been to make planless agriculture pay, not to bring the American farmers under the discipline of a real plan of production.

What, then, of industry? Were not the N.R.A. Codes a form of planning based on the idea of corporate industrial self-government? Doubtless they can be so regarded, if it is regarded as 'planning to institute in each industry a body entitled to regulate output and prices without providing for any sort of co-ordination between the decisions reached by the authorities for the separate industries, or taking any measures to ensure that on the whole the available resources of production shall be more fully employed. The N.R.A. Codes were perfect examples of restrictive sectional capitalist pseudo-planning, which may be effective in diminishing but cannot possibly increase the total employment of resources in production.

The special 'planning' measures applied to both agriculture and industry were thus entirely restrictive in their effects. For securing the fuller use of the available productive resources, the New Deal relied not on planning at all, but on monetary manipulation and the spending of public money. It was hoped that if the State went on pumping money into the banks, borrowers would appear to take advantage of it; and in order to make this more likely increased the supply of the Administration money in the pockets of the public in a host of ways—by paying out wages for Public Works, Civil Works, and relief, by subsidising farmers through the purchase of their crops at enhanced prices, by taking over farm and homestead mortgages, and thus putting the creditors of the farmers and home-owners back in funds, by lending money for house repair and construction, and, on a much larger scale, to the railroads, and so on. But not one of these measures except the first can by any stretch of imagination be regarded as making towards a planned economy. The object behind them was indeed that of increasing the total current demand for goods and services, but not that of planning in any way the nature of the output which was to arise in response to this increased demand.

But cannot Public Works and Civil Works, at any rate, be regarded as contributions to economic planning? Far from it. The Civil Works programme was no more than an attempt to set some millions of the unemployed doing something—doing anything—in preference to giving them relief without service in return. It was the most planless, chaotic and wasteful of all the enterprises of the New Deal. For the Federal Administration neither possessed nor attempted to establish any co-ordinating control over the hosts of State and local projects that were carried on under the name of Civil Works. What work was done with the aid of the money hardly anyone even pretended to care: the object of the Civil Works programme was not an increased production of useful things, but the circulation of additional money on terms that could be reconciled with the requirements of the American conscience. The giving of something for nothing was regarded by orthodox American opinion as grossly demoralising: the receiving of nothing for something was by comparison a thoroughly defensible procedure. As a contribution to economic planning the Civil Works programme can be dismissed with a caution.

What, then, of President Roosevelt's Public Works projects? These were at least selected with something of an eye to their possible usefulness; and they included a number of schemes which might well have formed part of an economic plan. But here again the conditions precluded any real planning; for projects had to be selected not on their real merits alone, but in such a way as to ration them out among States and to avoid any sort of competition that private business would be likely to resent. It is, however, obviously impossible to insert into an economy that is mainly unplanned more than a very limited number of useful projects that will not compete with one or another branch of unplanned private industry. Doubtless the administrators of the Public Works scheme did their best; but, under orders to find plenty of schemes in order to get more men into work and more money into circulation and at the same time to avoid all schemes to which business men could take exception on the ground of their competitive character, they were facing a plainly impracticable task. To plan work for the sake of employment and the circulation of money is not economic planning: it implies a situation which can exist at all only in a planless economy.

Of course, the vital question for the American people was not whether the New Deal was a step towards a planned economy, but whether it was likely to succeed in restoring production and employment. What I have been trying to show is that the methods on which President Roosevelt relied for the restoration of prosperity were almost purely monetary, the non-monetary elements in the New Deal being with few exceptions merely methods of alleviating the trouble and not of curing it. It may be said that this is not true of those parts of the Roosevelt programme which were concerned with 'reform' rather than 'recovery,' such as the restrictions on speculation in stocks and shares and the divorce of the deposit banks from their security affiliates. But these measures, while they might be of importance in checking a threatened boom, were obviously of no help in bringing about a capitalist revival. Again, it may be claimed that the attempt to raise wages under the N.R.A. was a non-monetary measure making for the improvement of consumers' demand. But the President's zeal for higher wages seems speedily to have ebbed when he discovered that their immediate effect on business activity was more likely to be deterrent than stimulating; and in fact the advances conceded under the N.R.A. at the outset were speedily swallowed up in the higher prices induced by the President's monetary and agricultural measures.

The New Deal, as an attempt to promote recovery, really stands or falls by the fate of the President's monetary policy. This, however, cuts two ways. The effect of putting additional money into circulation, by forms of public spending which do actually get it into the consumers' pockets, is undoubtedly stimulating to many forms of economic activity, especially those which minister directly to the consumers' demands. But if the business world regards the increase in the supply of money as 'unsound,' and doubts the continuance of consumers' demand at the higher level, the effect must be to damp down investment, and positively to reduce demand for the products of the industries producing capital goods. These, however, were the most depressed group, which the Administration was most anxious to revive. A stimulus could be given to them by extensive programmes of public works, which created a demand for their products. But this stimulus could only be temporary, and would disappear as soon as the volume of public works was reduced. It was no substitute, as a means to recovery, for a revival of the will to invest in capital goods on the part of the private *entrepreneurs*. Nor could it be a substitute, unless the Administration was prepared to invade the competitive field, and to replace the private investor permanently by setting up as a rival producer. But, of course, any attempt to do this would at once further undermine capitalist 'confidence' and cause private employers to begin discharging workers right and left.

It is nevertheless true that a boom can be created by monetary expansion, if it is pushed far enough. But, paradoxically, this can be achieved only at

AMERICAN 'PLANNING'—NEW DEAL 201

the risk of destroying capitalist confidence in the value of money, so that owners of money hasten to convert it into real things in preference to holding it unused. For, when a really inflationary situation develops, there is bound to be an investment boom. The ownership of real things, such as factories, is obviously preferable at such times to the ownership of money; and any *entrepreneur* who borrows money and converts it into capital goods can look forward to paying off his debt in depreciated currency, and having the capital goods for next to nothing. An investment boom of this sort happened in Germany during the post-war inflation. It would have happened in the United States if President Roosevelt had pushed on with monetary expansion to an unlimited extent.

But in order to reach a boom of this kind it would be necessary to pass through an intervening phase in which the waning of capitalist confidence would lead to a widespread discharge of workers and lessening of productive activity. The capitalists, before giving up their faith in the value of money, would make a stand against the inflationary movement by withdrawing their money from use, in the hope that their 'strike' action might suffice to stop the inflation. If the inflation were stopped, there would be left as its legacy a deep depression, out of which the climb-up would be bound to be slow and long, if it occurred at all. If, on the other hand, the inflation were continued all the more rapidly in order to counteract the capitalist 'strike,' a boom of sorts would follow. But this type of boom is inherently unstable and evanescent: it ends either, as the German inflation ended, in a virtually complete destruction of the value of money, which paralyses the entire economic system, or in a decisive reversal of policy, which at once inaugurates a deflationary preference for money to goods, and renders a large part of the productive machinery incapable of profitable use.

The United States is still far removed from an inflationary crisis of this kind. For the New Deal did not in fact take on an inflationary character. Despite intensive Government spending, there was no sensational increase in the volume of money in active circulation, largely because much of the new money that was poured out on government account was used not for additional spending but for the repayment of debts, and therefore went to strengthen bank reserves rather than to add to the active circulation. Some increase in the volume of circulation there was, over and above what went to balance the increase in total production; and this new money helped to raise prices. But the price-level showed no signs of getting out of hand, as it does when real inflation is in progress. Indeed, the difficulty was to push up commodity prices as fast as the Administration desired.

In effect, both Big Business and the Administration were torn between inconsistent desires. Big Business wanted both rapid recovery and business confidence, because it looked to the business man to take the initiative over again as soon as the required stimulus had been given. But the measures that seemed most calculated to promote employment were also those which were most certain to destroy business confidence. The Administration wanted to raise wages, because it saw that high purchasing power was essential to prosperity; but it also wanted to widen the margin between costs and profits, in order to persuade the business men to produce more. Big Business wanted a wider market for its products; but it also wanted low wages, in order to keep down costs. The Administration would have liked to reduce tariffs, in order to provide a bigger market for agricultural exports; but Big Business wanted high tariffs, in order to exclude competitive industrial imports.

In face of these contradictions the prophets of the New Deal halted uncertainly, or rather darted uncertainly to and fro from one expedient to another. They dared not resolve the contradictions, because any policy designed to resolve them would have undermined the foundations of the profit system. But neither dared they do nothing, lest a wave of popular distress and disillusionment should sweep them away. Consequently they continued to pour out money for public works and relief, and to use monetary manipulation as a means of promoting expansion, without pushing either of these methods to such extremes as seriously to alarm the business world. They could pursue this course for a long time; for, as long as there was no real threat of uncontrolled inflation, the business men were very ready to lend the Government money which they saw no prospect of using profitably themselves. But, though economic activity was to some extent increased by the outpouring of public funds, nothing could be done in this way to revive normal capitalist activity in the field of investment. The tonic was temporary in its effects; and any decrease in the dose administered threatened promptly to cause a recession.

The American situation thus very clearly illustrated the fundamental dilemma of Capitalism. It is possible that Mr. Hoover and his friends were right in asserting that, if President Roosevelt would only withdraw from the field and leave the familiar economic laws to assert their sway, recovery would come at last. But it would certainly have come only at the end of a prolonged and exceedingly painful orgy of liquidation and public distress, in the course of which there would have been a great many bankruptcies and evictions, a great deal of near-starvation, and almost certainly a great deal of rioting and even positive revolt. Things might

AMERICAN 'PLANNING'—NEW DEAL

have come right in the long run—in a capitalist sense. But would the sufferers have agreed to endure in quiet, while the capitalist remedies were working their painful magic? Is it not more likely that someone of the type of Senator Huey Long would have acquired the status of a national hero, and got power to outdo President Roosevelt in the adventurousness of his expedients? Fear of this made Big Business afraid to come to grips with the President, while fear of Big Business caused the President to resort to compromises which merely kept the system alive, without introducing any reforms capable of preventing a recurrence of crisis.

Under these conditions any real planning was out of the question. There can be no real planning without a planning authority empowered to lay down what shall be, as well as what shall not be, produced. But to prescribe what shall be produced is impossible under a system which places its reliance on the initiative of the profit-seeking *entrepreneur*; for no Government, however authoritarian, can for long compel the *entrepreneur* to go on producing at a loss. In a planned economy, the control of production is combined with the control of incomes, so that a balance can be struck on the basis of a full use of the available resources. But the profit-seeking *entrepreneur* will produce and invest only in accordance with the stimulus derived from his expectation of profit, and must behave in this way, under penalty of bankruptcy or failure if he does not.

Capitalist production of goods, in fact, is capable of being planned only in a restrictive sense, unless the State itself is prepared, by policies of re-armament or public works, to supply the deficiencies of consumers' demand. If the State is not to compete with the private *entrepreneur*, the only form of production that can be planned, except restrictively, is the production of money; for money stands in opposition to goods, and not in competition with them. But to plan the supply of money, in an expansionist sense, is a very different matter from planning the supply of goods. For money is the only 'product' of which the supply can be increased without subtracting productive resources from other uses. The labour used up in producing and printing paper money is negligible; and the addition to bank staffs caused by an increase in the amount of money in circulation is unimportant. The supply of money can be doubled, quadrupled, multiplied by a hundred, without any appreciable diminution in the supply of resources available for making other things.

But if the supply of money is increased, the new money must pass into somebody's hands for spending. Under the New Deal the additional money accrued in the first instance chiefly to the public authority itself as employer of workers on public and civil works, to farmers and other consumers by

AMERICAN 'PLANNING'—NEW DEAL 207

way of public grants and loans, and to contractors employed in the public service. From these recipients it passed on to others, some to be restored to the banks in repayment of loans and thus cancelled, and some to go on circulating from hand to hand as an addition to the current supply of purchasing power.

The wiser heads behind the Roosevelt policy realised that if this new money could be so infused into the circulation as to produce an even expansion in the money demand for all types of goods, its effect would be to promote an orderly expansion of output, not to the full extent of the addition to the supply of money, but to a less extent according to the rise in prices which it provoked. But, of course, the effect of the new money never could be an even expansion in all types of money demand. It was bound to cause, according to the manner in which it was first spent, different reactions on the productive system. In the American case, its chief effects were in the first place on the industries supplying materials for use in public works, and on the general mass of consumers' demand. It thus served to stimulate both the industries producing consumers' goods and some, but not all, of the industries producing capital goods. These were its first effects, and they were on the whole quite well distributed.

But the secondary effects are also important. From the original beneficiaries the money passed on to others—to workmen employed in the stimulated industries, to capitalist owners of these industries, to tradesmen who handled the increased sales, and to their employees, and so on. This second diffusion of purchasing power must evidently tend to follow the current general distribution of income in the community, save to the extent to which the improved money demand widened the surplus between costs and selling prices, and thus increased the *entrepreneurs'* share more than others'. The question that next arises is how this second diffusion of money must react on different types of demand.

It must clearly again raise the total of price-offers in the consumers' trades. But a part of it would be applied to paying off debts, and thus either cancelled, where the debt was ultimately to a bank, or transferred to 'savings.' A further part would be 'saved' by the recipients at every circulation of the money. If these savings were then invested in private business undertakings, the demand for the products of the capital goods industries would revive apart from Government orders, and the new capital goods would be used to expand the supply of consumers' goods, and to lower their costs. Revival would then be achieved, provided that the new capital goods did not provoke so rapid a displacement of labour as to re-create unemployment and bring about a renewed contraction of demand.

But what was to happen if the owners of the saved money refused to invest it in private enterprise, and either hoarded it or lent it only to the Government, in order that the Government might use it for fresh diffusions of purchasing power? If the money were hoarded, there would be no expansion of demand in the industries producing capital goods, and these would have to depend on fresh public orders for their continuance in production. Nor would there be any lowering of costs through the application of new capital instruments, so that the additional money-demand for consumers' goods would go largely to raise prices and not to expand real demand. Equally, if the money were lent to the Government, and invested only in non-competitive public works, the cost of producing consumers' goods would not fall, and the new money demand would raise prices rather than real demand.

But the willingness of the owners of money to invest privately in capital goods depends not on the current condition of consumers' demand but on estimates of its future course. Doubtless, a sharp rise in the prices of consumers' goods will always cause some fresh investment; but unless there is confidence in its continuance, the investment will be confined mainly to capital goods which can be brought quickly into use, and are relatively cheap, so that their cost can be quickly written off. Private investment beyond these limits depends on long-run estimates of demand, or in other words on business confidence in the future.

But will business men feel confidence in the situation which we are considering? They will not if there is any serious threat of radical legislation calculated to raise their costs of production. If they fear that higher wages and higher taxation are likely to eat up the larger margins currently in existence between costs and prices, they will hold back and refuse to invest, preferring to lend their savings to the Government at interest. The Government, therefore, will have to go on spending money on public works in order to save the capital goods industries from renewed collapse.

The question, then, for President Roosevelt was whether American business men could, or could not, be made to feel enough confidence in the future for investment to revive apart from the action of the State, and for more labour to be taken on by private industry. Undoubtedly, many business men, including especially the great financiers, felt a marked lack of confidence in the President. They suspected him of a desire, not merely to restore capitalism to prosperity, but also to reform its ways and subject it to some real amount of public control. They suspected him of favouring Trade Unions, to which they were hotly opposed; of meaning to tax the rich much more heavily, and use the money for the development of social services, to which

AMERICAN 'PLANNING'—NEW DEAL

they were also keenly hostile; and, last but not least, they suspected him of strong antipathy to themselves and to their immense political influence.

There were, however, other thoughts in their minds. Loudly as President Landon's supporters in 1936 denounced the President as a Bolshevik, they did not really believe a word of what they were saying. They were well aware that he was, in fact, as fervent a believer in the virtues of private capitalism as they were themselves—albeit he also believed in the reform of capitalism, which they did not. They had, therefore, at the back of their minds an idea that, even if they were fighting Roosevelt now, they might need to combine with him later on against forces much further to the left—against the rising force of radical Trade Unionism, represented by John L. Lewis and his Committee for Industrial Organisation, against currency cranks and financial demagogues of the brand of Coughlin and Townsend, and against all those chaotic left-wing forces which they were in the habit of lumping together in their minds as ' Communist.'

In these circumstances, the lack of confidence in President Roosevelt, even in the highest financial circles, did not go nearly so deep as they said it did. They wanted Roosevelt out, and Landon in, and they spent many millions of dollars on their highly unsuccessful campaign on Landon's behalf. But they did not at all want a renewed depression—both because Roosevelt, with all his faults, was undoubtedly enabling them to make a great deal of money, and because they were well aware that a renewal of the slump would immensely strengthen the forces standing a long way to the President's Left.

Accordingly, Big Business's lack of confidence in the New Deal did not prevent it from cashing it on the opportunities of profit which the New Deal offered. It did cause them to hang back at first from investing their money. But as the outpouring of purchasing power by the State brought about a greater and greater market revival, they were tempted back, grumbling, into the field of long-term investment—the more inevitably because there was nothing else they could do with the vast quantities of money that was being poured back into their hands as frozen debts were liquidated, and as the banks became choked with the money put into circulation by means of the Government's schemes. In the end, Big Business came into line with the revival, and for the time being the trick was done.

Big Business had an additional inducement to come in. The President, as we have seen, had to go on until he either succeeded or failed. He could not afford to stand still. But Big Business was by this time well aware, from plenty of hints which he himself had dropped, that in most directions of unorthodox experiment he had no desire to go any further than he was driven. As soon as recovery had reached generally satisfactory dimensions, the President was very willing to take a rest from his policy of 'trying everything once,' and to give the business world a chance to manage the rest for itself.

By the time of President Roosevelt's triumphant re-election in 1936, this stage had been reached. The President was already resting on what had been done, and refraining from new expedients during the campaign. He talked soothingly to Big Business, despite its acerbity against himself. When he was back in office, with an immense majority behind him, Big Business was ready enough to come to terms.

Why should it not be ready? Under the New Deal the greatest crisis in American economic history had been, from the capitalist point of view, brought successfully to an end, in such a way as to leave the capitalist system intact, despite the mass of anti-capitalist feeling that had been aroused. Prices had risen as a result of the expansion of monetary circulation: profits were back in most industries at a highly satisfactory level; and the old game of stock market speculation had been resumed pretty much in the old ways. Money, it is true, was still being poured out in work-relief and farm subsidies of many kinds; for recovery had neither absorbed nearly all the unemployed nor got the farmers at all completely out of their financial difficulties. But the business world was not much worried by these imperfections, which did not interfere with its return to the familiar practices of money-making, and indeed helped it by increasing the volume of effective consumers' demand.

Does this experience show that, despite all that was said and written during the years after the Wall Street crash of 1929, there was nothing fundamentally wrong with American capitalism after all? It does refute those who thought they saw, in the troubles of the American business world after 1929, the onset of the final crisis of American capitalism. Capitalism, in America as in Great Britain, is tough enough to survive even such crises as that of the past few years without needing even to invoke Fascism to save it, as long as it is not confronted with any formidable Socialist movement, embodying a practicable alternative to its continuance. By monetary expansion, accompanied by sufficient State measures of public works or relief to get more money into active circulation, capitalism can boost itself back to prosperity, of a sort, without even needing to abrogate the forms of democratic government. It needs to resort to Fascism as a means of protecting its property only where there is a Socialist movement strong enough to threaten its very existence. Capitalism can recover from the severest crisis if there is no movement strong enough to offer the prospect of replacing it by an alternative system. It may be driven to the use of unorthodox expedients which its leaders cordially dislike. But it can recover, because it contains within itself the conditions of recovery as well as of depression.

In the absence of State action to foster recovery by unorthodox means, the instrument of recovery is wholesale liquidation. Gradually, under pressure of the crisis, the 'unfit,' by capitalist standards, are weeded out. The 'redundant' capital accumulated during the preceding period of boom is put out of action, and written off as lost. Stocks of unsold goods are gradually dispersed. New inventions provide fresh incentives to capital investment, even in a market which is generally depressed. After immense sufferings have been inflicted on those who are not rich enough to ride out of the crisis with the aid of their reserves, things begin to mend; and the improvement, when it has begun, becomes cumulative, till capitalist society advances again towards another boom—with another crisis to follow.

The danger of waiting for recovery to come in this orthodox, highly unpleasant fashion is that the suffering involved in it may be so acute that people will resort to revolution rather than endure it. America, in 1933 and 1934, might easily have gone revolutionary, if there had been any party or movement capable of taking the lead in a revolutionary crusade. If this had existed, and the revolutionary movement had assumed serious dimensions, counter-revolution, financed with all the resources of the American rich, would at once have been organised against it. There would have been bloody conflict, ending either in some sort of Socialism or in Fascist dictatorship—for how else could it have ended if it had once begun?

There was, however, no revolutionary leadership. But the danger of such a leadership coming into being was too great for American capitalism merely to wait for economic recovery to arrive of itself, as a result of deflation and liquidation on the grand scale. So at any rate felt President Roosevelt and the mass of his active supporters outside the die-hard ranks of American Big Business and finance. Accordingly monetary expansion was tried; and, when that was plainly ineffective by itself, money was poured into the consumers' pockets by way of public works, subsidies and relief payments of any and every sort. In due course recovery came, without the wholesale liquidation which would otherwise have been involved—and without civil war.

There is, however, no reason at all to suppose that the New Deal, in helping the United States to weather the crisis of 1929 and the following years, has achieved anything which will prevent a recurrence of such crises. For the American economic system has not been planned or reformed in any durable way. It has been tided over the crisis at vast expense; and it is now being set free to resume its old methods of speculative profit-making practically without hindrance or control. Something has indeed been done to put the banking system on a sounder capitalist basis, by disentangling the deposit banks from direct participation in stock market gambling. A little has been done towards providing the American workers with social services such as exist in the more advanced capitalist countries of Europe. But these changes only touch the fringe of the American business system, with its marked propensity to the extremes of speculative excess.

On the other hand, recovery is at present far from complete. Unemployment continues on a large scale, and still calls for emergency measures of relief. Farm prices have been restored only at the cost of greatly reduced production, which leaves a large part of the farm population redundant and still in dependence on public doles. America, for the first time in her history, seems to be carrying a permanent surplus of labour. This will tend to make the next crisis worse when it comes, as there is every reason to expect that come it will.

As for planning, there is already little enough of it left. For President Roosevelt set out, not to plan for the future, but to tide over present difficulties by emergency measures. The American economy, after the New Deal, remains almost as planless as it was before the crisis began.

CHAPTER V

CAPITALIST 'PLANNING' IN GREAT BRITAIN

AMONG the leading industrial countries, Great Britain was up to 1914, and even in most respects up to 1918, the outstanding example of *laissez-faire* in practice. Up to 1914 foreign trade was unfettered by any sort of State control; apart from a few revenue duties, importers and exporters were free to carry in and out of the country exactly what goods they pleased. The movement of capital was similarly uncontrolled; and every year a substantial part of the new investments of British capitalists were made abroad, either in Empire or in foreign countries. Financially, Great Britain operated under the gold standard, which fixed the value of British currency in relation to the currencies of the other leading countries, and left the Bank of England to adapt the supply of credit to the state of the foreign exchanges, under a system which was operated by fixed rules and came near to being automatic in its working.

Home production, like foreign trade, was left to look after itself. Beyond prescribing certain minimum conditions of employment under the Factory and Mines Acts and laying down minimum rates of wages for a few sweated trades, the State left both industry and agriculture to their own devices. There was not even any attempt to deal by legislation with the problem of combines and monopolies. Great Britain had no anti-trust legislation such as existed in the United States. There had been, indeed, under the Liberal Governments which held office from 1906 to 1914 some extension of the social services, accompanied by a very limited attempt to supplement the incomes of the poor by taxing the rich. But this attempt had not gone far. It can be said with a very close approximation to truth that up to 1914 Great Britain furnished an almost perfect example of a planless economy—of the working of the economic system in accordance with the ' natural laws ' beloved of the classical economists.

This freedom could not, of course, survive the experience of war. While the war lasted, production had to be directed to meeting war needs, and the Government, as the principal customer of many of the producers and the principal claimant on the available supplies of labour, inevitably acquired an extensive power over industry and agriculture. The Ministries of Munitions, Food, Agriculture and National Service necessarily assumed large authority over what was to be produced. They could grant or withhold supplies of labour or of materials to firms working for private customers; and they were

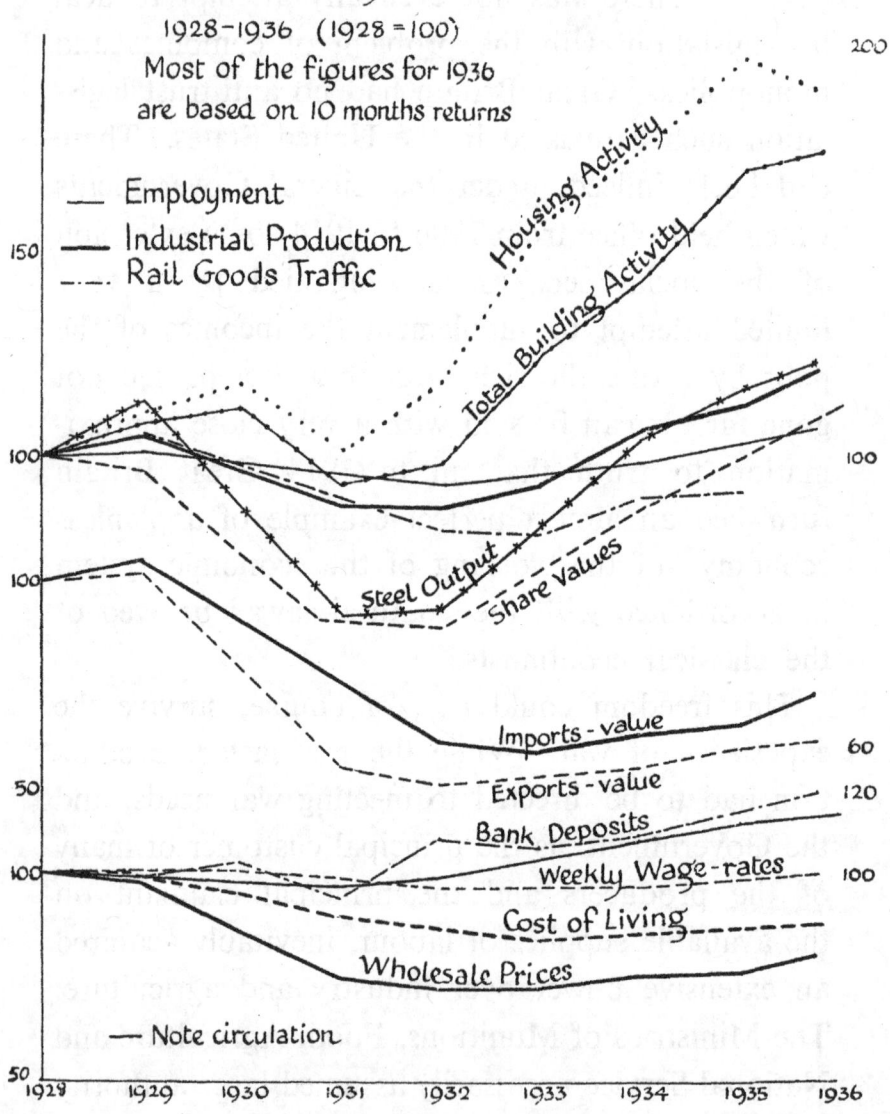

ECONOMIC ACTIVITY IN GREAT BRITAIN, 1928–1936
(1928 = 100)

	1929	1930	1931	1932	1933	1934	1935	1936	
Industrial Production	106	98	89	88	94	105	112	121	(9 months)
Output of Steel	113	86	61	62	82	104	116	122	(10 months)
Building Activity, Total	108	111	93	98	124	142	169	174	(,,)
Housing Activity	110	117	101	117	155	173	195	188	(,,)
Rail Traffic, Ton-miles	106	100	92	83	84	91	92	—	
Employment	102	98	94	94	97	100	104	108	(,,)
Net Imports—Value	103	89	74	61	58	63	65	73	(,,)
Net Exports—Value	101	79	54	50	51	55	59	61	(,,)
Wholesale Prices	97	85	74	72	72	75	76	80	(,,)
Cost of Living	99	95	89	86	84	85	86	88	(,,)
Weekly Wage-rates	100	100	98	96	95	96	97	100	(9 months)
Industrial Share Values	98	79	61	59	73	88	99	113	
Note Circulation	98	97	96	98	104	107	112	114	(10 months)
Bank Deposits	98	101	94	108	106	108	114	119	(,,)

themselves, in conjunction with other Ministries, giving, as the war advanced, more and more of the orders which producers were called upon to fulfil,

Wherever possible, the war-time Governments, true to the traditions of private enterprise, exercised their new authority through the agency of the business men actually engaged in the various trades. There grew up a host of executive and advisory committees, composed for the most part of business men, whose task it was to mobilise industry and agriculture for war service. In order to facilitate dealings, the State encouraged business men to combine. It entered into treaties with representative capitalists in each industry, and left them as free as it could to devise their own measures for meeting the national needs. Above all, it left them free to make enormous profits, even after the special war-time taxes had been paid.

Under war conditions, foreign trade necessarily ceased to be free; for producers could apply to producing for foreign markets only resources which the Government did not require for itself, and both imports and exports came under State control on account of the growing shortage of shipping space occasioned by submarine warfare and the requisitioning of tonnage for war purposes. British foreign trade declined sharply, and countries which had looked largely to Great Britain for the supply of manufactured goods were compelled to seek

CAPITALIST 'PLANNING' IN BRITAIN 223

other sources of supply or to develop their own industries, even on a less economic basis. It became clear that, when the war ended, Great Britain would not be able simply and automatically to resume her old place in the trade of the world.

Moreover, the export of capital ceased abruptly; for all the available supply of savings, and much more, was swallowed up in financing the war. Great Britain, from being the world's greatest lender, became a borrower of capital, chiefly from the United States, whence came a flood of war imports unbalanced by exports from Great Britain. Past overseas investments had, to a substantial extent, to be sold in America to pay for foodstuffs and munitions of war.

The gold standard went for the time by the board. The sterling–dollar exchange was first managed by means of loans raised through Morgan's by the British Government, and then officially ' pegged,' when the United States came into the war on the side of the Allies. The pound lost its link with gold: a managed currency perforce replaced the old nearly automatic system.

Under stress of war feeling, the first breaches were made in the system of Free Trade. Protective duties were imposed on a few commodities in the interests of home development. But protection could not be of much importance while the war lasted; for imports and exports were regulated by the exigencies of shipping space.

By 1918, in these and other ways, the British economic system had become in effect a 'planned economy'—planned for maximum production with the limited supply of labour left by the draining away of workers to the armed forces, planned to meet the needs to war.

This form of planning, however, could not survive the return of peace. It depended essentially on three things—the Government's position as a huge-scale buyer of products, the war-induced shortage of labour and materials, and the rationing of shipping space. As soon as the war ended, the huge Government orders for war supplies came abruptly to an end. The supply of labour was rapidly increased by the return of workers from the armed forces. Shipping space, especially after the confiscation of the German mercantile marine, became embarrassingly abundant in face of the slow recovery of international trade in a war-impoverished world.

Under these changed conditions, there was a scamper back to 'business as usual.' The State gave up, as fast as it could, the controls which had been imposed on industry and agriculture during the war. Business men were left to re-adjust their methods to the changed economic demands of the post-war world. Everywhere, a determined attempt was made to get back as nearly as possible to the conditions which had existed before the war. The only significant exception that was deliberately made was the retention of the war-time protective duties designed to 'safeguard' certain home industries.

But the return to 'normality' could not be effected in all cases without a good deal of delay. Much against its will, the State had to keep certain controls in being. Coal control ended only in 1921 to the accompaniment of a bitter industrial struggle. The gold standard could not be restored until 1925.

By stages, however, Great Britain did return almost completely to the old conditions of *laissez-faire*. Tariffs applied only to a narrow range of goods, and Mr. Baldwin's desire, in 1923, to adopt a general tariff, led to a crushing electoral defeat. When in 1925 Mr. Churchill had restored the gold standard at the pre-war gold value of sterling, and the pound was again 'looking the dollar in the face,' Great Britain stood formally, in economic policy, not very far from where she had stood in 1914.

But the restored system did not work in the old way. Some of the foreign markets lost during the war were never regained. The cotton industry, by far the most important British export trade, never recovered its old prosperity. The coal trade had only a fleeting glimpse of its old greatness in 1923 and 1924; and that was due to the French occupation of the Ruhr, and not to economic conditions. From the moment of the post-war slump, the number of workers unemployed in Great Britain never fell below a million; and there were always 'depressed areas' unable to lift themselves out of adversity by any effort of their own.

Between 1925 and 1931 much of the blame for this state of things was laid at the door of those who had mistakenly restored the gold standard at the pre-war parity of the pound and the dollar. It was easy to see that the pound was 'overvalued,' and that its overvaluation was seriously hampering the exporters. There were some who argued that it had been a mistake to go back at all to the gold standard, and that a 'managed currency' would have served much better the interests of trade and industry; while others held merely that the pound should have been valued less highly in terms of gold. At all events, the overvaluation of sterling imposed on Great Britain a deflationary financial policy, designed to bring down prices by compressing wages and other costs. But costs were not easy to compress. Interest rates were kept high both by monetary scarcity and by the existence of a huge mass of Government debt bearing high rates and due to mature at an early date. And, in face of high rates of interest, the workers were not disposed readily to allow the entire burden of reducing costs to be placed upon them.

Conditions, then, were not at all comfortable in Great Britain even before the onset of the world depression. But the depression, from the moment

CAPITALIST 'PLANNING' IN BRITAIN   227

of the Wall Street panic of 1929, inevitably made matters much more difficult. As slump conditions developed in one country after another, British exports underwent a sharp decline. Prices fell rapidly, above all prices of foodstuffs and raw materials. For the demand of raw materials was sharply reduced by the American depression; while foodstuffs are produced under conditions which make it exceedingly difficult to reduce supply in face of failure of demand.

After 1929, Great Britain, as the world's great free market for imports of most kinds, felt the full impact of the world's desire to sell at almost any price. Immediately, this benefited the British consumers—or rather those of them who had incomes wherewith to buy. The cost of living fell rapidly, and imports into Great Britain remained high in face of the fall in exports. By 1931, instead of being left with a substantial balance of capital to send abroad after paying for imports, Great Britain was confronted with a large adverse balance of payments.

There need have been nothing very alarming about this, if it could have been regarded as merely temporary; for there was fully enough British capital invested at short term overseas to stand the strain. There might even have been no British crisis, had not the difficulties of sterling coincided with the presence in office of a Labour Government unloved by the financial interests. As matters were, something of a panic set in. The Labour Government, refusing as a body to take the orders given to it by the Bank of England, was driven from office; and its leader, MacDonald, came back at the head of a Tory-Liberal coalition with a mission to 'save the pound and the country.'

During the next few months British economic policy underwent a complete transformation. There were, broadly, two obvious ways of setting about the task of redressing the balance of payments. One was to check imports by means of a protective tariff; the other was to reduce the gold value of the pound. The incoming Government promptly adopted both expedients. Great Britain, the classic home of Free Trade, went over holus-bolus to a system of complete protection. Great Britain, the world's financial centre and the greatest upholder of the gold standard, went over to an unfixed system which in fact involved the institution of a 'managed currency.'

Now, any tariff that discriminates between commodities and has a protective purpose involves some degree of economic planning. The Import Duties Advisory Committee which was set up to administer the new British tariff necessarily became a body empowered to foster certain industries as against others; and it was a natural enough extension of its powers when, in the case of the steel industry, it was given the task of insisting on a certain degree of reorganisation as a condition of granting tariff protection. To be sure, its conditions were by no means onerous; but they at least embodied the principle of the State's right to have a say in the policies and methods of any industry to which it conceded its assistance against foreign competitors.

Before long, the wider implications of the new British commercial policy began to become plain. The Dominions, though no duties had been imposed by Great Britain upon their products, took fright at the possibility of the tariff being extended to them, and began to demand a larger share of the British market at the expense of foreign suppliers. At Ottawa the Dominions drove hard bargains with the Mother Country, selling their own tariff preferences to British producers as dear as they could in exchange for an increasing command of the British market. The Ottawa Agreements in turn alarmed Denmark and Argentina. Great Britain had to make up her mind how much of her food supply she meant to produce at home, how much to buy from the Dominions in exchange for British exports, and how much to continue to draw from foreign countries.

All this time the British farmers, having to meet the competition of cheap imports of food from overseas, were clamouring for protection. Most agricultural imports had been excluded from the tariff introduced after the crisis of 1931; for the

Government was afraid of the outcry which would be provoked by any attempt to tax the people's food. Nor could such taxation have done much for the British farmer if Dominion produce had been excepted. Certain luxury and semi-luxury foodstuffs were indeed subjected to taxation in 1931; but the great basic commodities remained untaxed.

This did not mean that the State was doing nothing for the farmers. Before the world depression began, the arable farmers had been aided by a subsidy on sugar-beet—a most expensive subsidy, which actually cost more than would have sufficed to buy the sugar abroad. To this had been added by the Labour Government the Wheat Act of 1930 and the Agricultural Marketing Act of 1930. Under the Wheat Act, flour millers were compelled to purchase 'quota certificates' from other buyers who were using more than the required 'quota' of home-grown wheat. Moreover, the farmers were enabled to sell their wheat at a price much in excess of its market value, the amount of the subsidy being recovered from the public in the price of bread. In order that this subsidy might not cause a big extension of the area under wheat, the total sum to be distributed was fixed, so that the amount of the bounty to the farmers per bushel fell as the quantity produced increased.

The Agricultural Marketing Act of 1930, on the other hand, gave neither subsidy nor protection.

It was an attempt by the Labour Government to induce the farmers to form co-operative marketing organisations by holding out to them the bait of compulsory powers. The producers of any agricultural commodity were empowered, subject to the approval of their scheme by the Ministry of Agriculture, to form a Marketing Board, to which all producers could be compelled to belong. The Board could then regulate prices and conditions of sale of the product.

Dr. Addison, the Labour Minister of Agriculture, fully intended to follow up this original Act with another, for the compulsory organisation of distribution, in the hope of narrowing the gap between the price paid by the consuming public and the farmers' receipts. But the Labour Government fell from office before it had time to carry out this complementary part of its programme; and the Act carried into law by Major Elliot, Dr. Addison's successor, followed quite different lines, obviously influenced by the flood of cheap imports which was seeking to find an outlet in Great Britain as a consequence of the world slump. Instead of attempting to reduce the wastes of distribution, Major Elliot, in the Agricultural Marketing Act of 1933, took power to regulate the importation of agricultural produce by the imposition of quantitative restrictions, and thus armed himself with the means of raising British agricultural prices by restricting imported supplies.

One weakness of this system was that it exacted, in tolls upon the consumers, a good deal more than it gave to the farmers. For the quantitative limitation enabled the importers to raise their prices much more than a tariff would have done; and the consumer had thus to pay more for both the home and the imported product. This happened especially in the case of bacon, in which the Danish producers held an advantage in quality. The price of Danish bacon rose by so much as a result of the restrictions that, after its enforcement, the Danes were actually receiving a larger aggregate sum than before in return for a greatly reduced quantity of bacon. Home output was increased; but inevitably the higher prices checked consumption.

Meanwhile, serious difficulties were arising over imports of beef and veal. British meat fell to prices which the farmers claimed to be ruinous to them, and the Government was driven to offer cattle-growers a temporary subsidy out of taxation, while it took time to consider its long-run policy. What the Government wanted to do was to impose a 'levy' on all imports of beef or veal, including supplies coming from .the Dominions, and to use the proceeds to pay for the subsidy which the cattle-raisers were to receive.

This course, however, met with strong opposition both on the part of the Dominions, which demanded free entry for their products, and on that of Argentina, which saw itself threatened with gradual exclusion of its goods. While attempts were being made to adjust these difficulties, the subsidy to the home-producers was continued on a temporary footing, and temporary agreements for quantitative restriction of imports were made with both the Dominions and Argentina. Not till the end of 1936 was the British Government in a position to announce its promised 'long-term policy.'

The policy, when it did come, proved to be merely one of continued subsidies to the home producers, to be partly financed by means of a levy, *alias* a duty, on the imports of foreign but not on those of Dominion meat. The Government had to abandon its proposal to tax Dominion imports, principally because Argentina could not be induced to agree to a rate of levy exceeding the preference already promised to the Dominions. This was to some extent an advantage; for it limited the extent to which the poorer consumers could be made to pay directly for the subsidy granted to the producers of the more expensive home-grown meat.

The Agricultural Marketing Acts were applied at an early stage to milk. In this instance the position was that practically all medical opinion laid great stress on the need for larger consumption of liquid milk, especially among the poorer sections of the people. There was also a recognised need for an improvement in quality, with a view to the elimination of sources of disease. British producers had a natural monopoly of the liquid milk market; but at current prices the liquid milk market did not absorb the entire supply, the balance being used for manufacture of condensed milk or of dairy produce, such as cheese and butter. Milk used for manufacture fetched lower prices than milk for liquid consumption.

Before the advent of the Milk Marketing Board, the producers in some areas were able to sell practically the whole of their supply for liquid consumption, whereas those in the remoter districts had to get rid of a large 'surplus' in the manufacturing market. The producers in liquid milk districts had to a substantial extent succeeded by scientific feeding in reducing seasonal variations in supply, which were much greater in other areas.

The world depression, among its other consequences, had brought about a very sharp fall in the prices of imported milk products. This drove down the prices at which 'surplus' milk could be sold for manufacture in Great Britain, and threatened the solvency of the producers who depended on the manufacturing market. The Milk Marketing Board, in order to help these producers, compelled all producers of milk (except a small number supplying tuberculin-tested milk) to sell their output through the Board at prices fixed by it. The Board was then responsible for disposing of what it could in the

CAPITALIST 'PLANNING' IN BRITAIN 235

liquid market, and getting rid of what remained at the very low prices obtainable from the manufacturers. This meant that, if the farmers were to receive remunerative prices, the consumers of liquid milk had to pay more in order to make up for the low prices paid by the manufacturers.

But high prices for liquid milk were plainly inconsistent with the increased liquid consumption which the scheme was supposed to bring about. They were bound to restrict consumption; and at the same time the favourable prices paid to farmers in more remote areas were bound to increase supply. Under the scheme supply did increase rapidly; but in face of the high liquid milk prices this meant that a larger and larger surplus had to be sold to manufacturers at a loss.

This situation was so absurd that something had to be done about it, especially as medical opinion was pressing more strongly than ever the needs of children for more fresh milk. The outcome was the 'Milk in Schools' scheme, under which a limited quantity of milk was supplied at a low price to school children during term, and some of the 'surplus' was thus diverted from the manufacturing market at a wholesale price intermediate between the price of liquid milk and that of milk destined for manufacture. But this scheme touched only the fringe of the problem, and up to the end of 1936 the main problem, that of making milk cheaper for the main body of the poorer consumers, remained wholly unsolved.

I have given these instances in order to show how, under capitalist conditions, the attempt to expand production is apt to hit up immediately against insoluble contradictions. Under the profit system, production can be expanded only by offering the producers higher prices. But consumption can be increased only by offering the consumers lower prices. British agricultural policy during the past few years has been conducted definitely with the object of raising farm prices. This has involved charging the consumers more than they would otherwise have had to pay, and has thus restricted consumption. But except where the home producers possess a natural monopoly, as in the case of liquid milk, the consumers cannot be charged more unless imports are restricted. Hence the tariffs, levies and quantitative restrictions on agricultural imports.

There is, of course, another way. Producers can get more without consumers paying more if the State is prepared to grant a subsidy out of the taxes. This was done, before the world slump, in the case of beet-sugar. But since the slump the State has shown, first in the Wheat Act and subsequently in other agricultural schemes, a marked preference for making the consumers pay, even when the restrictive effects on consumption have been perfectly plain. That it has been possible to do this without provoking a general outcry has been due to the very great fall in the prices of imported foodstuffs during the slump. In face of this fall, the State has been able to levy toll on the consumers without calling upon them to pay higher prices than they had been used to paying before the slump set in. But, as world agricultural prices recover, this becomes increasingly difficult. Already, at the end of 1936, under the combined influence of rising world prices and of national price-raising schemes, the cost of food at retail had risen by nearly 20 per cent since the middle of 1933.

Meanwhile in industry tariffs, without quantitative restrictions on imports or other devices for price-raising, were for the most part deemed sufficient help for the capitalist producers, whose power to export was of course stimulated by the decline in the gold value of sterling. But in certain industries special steps were taken to raise prices against the consumers. The Labour Government set the ball rolling with the Coal Mines Act of 1930, which endowed the colliery owners with power to fix selling prices and to restrict supplies. The aim of the Labour Government was doubtless mainly to improve miners' wages and hours; but the effect was to enable the colliery owners to carry on without the fundamental reorganisation of ownership and methods which the industry requires. In effect, the Act of 1930 compelled the home consumers of coal to subsidise the highly competitive export trade; and the attempt to make some sort of reorganisation a condition of the scheme was entirely defeated by the inadequacy of the powers given to the Coal Mines Reorganisation Commission established under the Act. This failure was not, indeed, wholly the Government's fault; for the House of Lords so amended the Bill as to make it impossible for the Commission to achieve any result. The upshot was that the colliery owners were placed in a position of legally entrenched monopoly against the public—a position which they still enjoy, and are unlikely to lose as long as the present Government remains in power.

The second industry which has been accorded special protection, beyond the tariff, is steel. In this instance, however, the tariff has been the main instrument. The steel producers were offered an all-round protection against imports on condition that they should take steps to reorganise their industry. They did not do this; but they did form a combination powerful enough to represent them very effectively. They then proceeded to negotiate with the continental steel producers, who were combined in the International Steel Cartel, for a mutual agreement for the allocation of markets. The foreign producers at once raised the question of their imports into Great Britain, which were considerable in the case of cheap raw steel. The

British body, dominated by the raw steel producers, offered an import quota entirely unsatisfactory to the Continental Cartel. At this point the discussions would have broken down had not the State come to the help of the British producers by agreeing to impose a prohibitively high 'bargaining' tariff on imported steel, with the direct object of bringing the foreigners to heel. This step was effective. Foreign steel was restricted to a small quantity in comparison with what had been coming in, not by a quota enforced by law, but by a private agreement between the British and the foreign capitalists. This was done in face of the protests of a number of steel-finishing firms, on which it imposed the necessity of buying their semi-finished materials, whether home-produced or imported, at considerably higher prices.

While these negotiations were going on, the British Government were endeavouring to stimulate British exports, and especially exports of coal, by means of a revised system of trade agreements with foreign countries. Denmark, in order to maintain the position of her goods in the British market, which is vital to her, was compelled to agree to buy a much larger proportion of her imports from Great Britain. A similar policy was followed, on a less extensive scale, with Norway and Sweden and other European countries, and later with Argentina. This method of bilateral bargaining has not indeed been pushed nearly so far by Great Britain as by Germany; but it has gone far enough, in conjunction with the creation and extension of the sterling currency area, to have a substantial effect in diverting the channels of British overseas trade.

The growth of the sterling area has, however, undoubtedly been a much more important factor than the new policy in respect of trade agreements, which largely depends upon it. When Great Britain went off the gold standard in 1931, it was widely prophesied that the lapse would lose London its cherished status as the financial centre of the world. But in fact the consequence has been to strengthen London's position. The United States, in the throes of a far deeper crisis, was in no condition to lay claim to London's inheritance, either before or after the dollar's fall from its high estate. France and other countries which remained on gold, so far from being strengthened, were greatly weakened by the necessity of pursuing violently deflationary policies. Gold might silt up in Paris; but it could not be used. As other countries, headed by Scandinavia and Australasia, followed sterling off the gold standard, Great Britain became the centre of a currency area whose members were free to adopt policies of monetary expansion in order to combat the crisis.

At first, it looked as if the pound sterling, having lost its fixed gold equivalent, would be left to find its own international level, with almost no 'management' by the British monetary authorities. But Britain's position as the centre of the sterling area and the continual and growing uncertainty about the future of other currencies soon made it desirable to resort to some sort of management. This was done by means of the Exchange Equalisation Fund, instituted under Government control, and not under the Bank of England, as an instrument for regularising currency fluctuations. The Fund, by transactions in foreign currencies and in gold, was able to build up reserves which gave it the power, over a short period, to do virtually what it pleased with the foreign exchanges; and this power was modified only when the United States, followed later by Holland and France, set up a similar Fund of its own. Thereafter, the foreign exchanges had to be managed collaboratively, by mutual agreement between the agencies controlling the various Funds. But their power was such as to make currency speculation much too risky a field for the private speculator.

Of course, no Exchange Equalisation Fund can stand out indefinitely against a long-term tendency to alter currency ratios. If any Fund were used to do this, it would in the end be stripped of its holdings of gold and foreign exchange, however large these might be. What an Exchange Fund can do is to stand out against short-term tendencies. If a long-term tendency towards a change of ratios exists, either the exchange rates must be allowed to alter, or internal monetary conditions must be adapted, much in the same way as under the gold standard, so as to reverse the trend. The existence of several Equalisation Funds, potentially capable of being operated one against another, makes the second method the more likely to be used. To a certain extent, as a result of this situation, Great Britain is already back on an international monetary standard, and under the necessity of adapting her internal credit policy to world conditions. But fortunately, as matters stand, this has involved no deflation; for other countries are also following in general a policy of expansion.

In sum, Great Britain, as a result of the changes made since 1929, has departed a long distance from the almost entirely planless economy of the years before the slump. She possesses to-day a managed currency, a largely managed foreign trade, a considerably managed system of agricultural production, and a managed system of industrial production extending to coal and steel. Add to these a partly managed house-building policy, under which the amount of public building is to some extent dovetailed in with the amount of private building that can be stimulated by lowered rates of interest. Add further the development of the 'grid' under the Central Electricity Board, the reorganisation of London passenger transport under the London Passenger Transport Board, and the small measures of assistance towards the production of oil from coal and the development of Trading Estates in certain of the derelict areas.

All this adds up to a quite formidable total of State intervention in industry. It has taken British economic life a long way from the old conditions of *laissez-faire*. But emphatically it does not add up to the institution of any real system of economic planning.

There are two main reasons why it does not. In the first place, it has all been done piecemeal, without co-ordination and to all appearance without any clear objective in view. The Government has tackled certain outstanding problems, as they have become too pressing to be let alone. But there are many more problems—the reorganisation of the cotton industry for example—which it has simply failed to tackle at all, and many—such as the restoration of the derelict areas—which it has handled in a quite ludicrously inadequate way. It has done only what it had to do—with the single exception of the resort to a general tariff on imports —under pressure from interests of which it has been compelled to take notice. This being its method of action, it has seldom considered the reaction of any one thing it has done on any other, or on the British economy as a whole.

Secondly, its expedients have been almost all in some sense restrictive—even when their declared purpose has been to expand production and employment. This is clearest of all in its agricultural schemes, which have been of such a nature as to increase home production only by bringing about a more than balancing contraction of imported supplies. It is hardly less clear in the case of coal and steel. From the standpoint of the consumers, the entire policy has been one of restriction of supplies in order to maintain producers' profits.

This stricture does not, indeed, apply to the Government's monetary policy. British monetary policy up to 1931 was severely deflationary; but since the suspension of the gold standard it has been moderately expansionist. This it is, and not any part of the 'planning' of trade or production, that has been responsible for the marked recovery of the years 1935 and 1936.

I am not saying that, in view of its assumptions, the Government could well have behaved in any other way. For, as I have pointed out earlier, money is the one commodity of which capitalism can expand the supply without making its issue unprofitable. This is because money has, for all practical purposes, no cost of production. Monetary expansion may lower interest rates, but it may at the same time increase the total sum paid in interest on the larger amount lent—lent at hardly any

CAPITALIST 'PLANNING' IN BRITAIN 245

additional cost to the ultimate lenders. In the case of no other commodity do even faintly similar conditions prevail. Real goods and services can be made more profitable to their producers, at any rate in periods of depression, only by restricting supply. There may be a few exceptions, when a commodity is made under conditions of rapidly decreasing cost in face of a highly elastic demand. But such cases are rare, and rarest in time of depression. The broad generalisation holds.

The experience of Great Britain since 1931 therefore goes to show two things. It shows that planning under capitalism, as far as it relates directly to production and trade, is unavoidably restrictive from the standpoint of the consumers, and almost invariably sectional and unco-ordinated. It is restrictive, because under capitalism recovery can come only from a revived expectation of profit; and it is sectional, because it approaches each part of the problem from the standpoint of the particular interests whose expectations of profit it is desired to stimulate.

But evidently no aggregate of sectional, restrictive ' plans ' can add up so as to constitute a planned economy. In effect, they do not add up at all; for one sectional plan is very apt to run counter to another. Planning, in any real sense, means planned use of the available productive resources in order to promote maximum consumption. It means an attempt to use more resources, and not less, and to use them in such a way as to further an end held to be socially desirable. By this test British 'planning,' as it has been developed since 1931, lamentably fails.

Yet the British economy has made, under this restrictive, anti-social system, a remarkable general recovery, from the capitalist point of view. This recovery has indeed left the problem of the derelict areas and of the great disorganised industries of coal and cotton almost untouched; but elsewhere there has been a very considerable revival. What I am contending is that this revival has been due, in part of course to world forces making for recovery, of which the British consumers have reaped the advantage, but, as far as it is attributable to any British action, to the one aspect of British policy which has not been restrictive in its effects. This is monetary expansion.

It is, however, clear that monetary expansion will not carry us much further than we have gone already. In 1936, the housing boom, based on low rates of interest, had already passed its peak, with the exhaustion in many areas of the demand for houses of the types which speculative builders found it profitable to build. Activity in capital works of construction, prompted largely by rearmament, was preventing any serious decline in the total volume of building activity. But, with this shift, the British economy like the German, though still to a smaller extent, was becoming dependent on rearmament as a necessary factor in maintaining industrial activity. In agriculture the dilemma that production could be stimulated only by high prices, whereas consumption could be increased only by lower prices, was becoming more and more obvious as the various marketing schemes worked themselves out in practice. The Government stared helplessly at the problem of the depressed areas, because in their case it was out of the question to stimulate activity by making their products dear, and no alternative solution came within the ambit of Cabinet Ministers' economic notions. Recovery existed, on a large scale; but it was both incomplete and very precarious, because the structure of production was being twisted to fit both a quite abnormal world situation and an activity in the armaments industries which would be clearly ruinous if it were long maintained, and destructive of employment and profit if it were quickly given up.

But, it may be said, surely the producers must be fairly paid for their toil and trouble; and therefore the Government was right to make their products dearer, when at existing prices it was clear that their returns were too low. In reply to that, I have admitted that a Government which believed in the universal value of the profit motive could not easily have behaved in any other way. There was indeed one thing it could have done, and in practice decisively refused to do. That was, to tackle the problem of distributive costs. This was what Dr. Addison meant to do in agriculture, as a sequel to the original Marketing Act. But Major Elliot, instead of taking up Dr. Addison's second projected Bill, adopted the restrictive policy of limiting imports in order to maintain home prices.

It is common knowledge that, in face of a sharp fall in the wholesale prices of both raw and manufactured goods, the costs of distribution have remained obstinately high. Why, then, at any rate in the case of food, has Dr. Addison's policy not been pursued? The answer is obvious. The distributive interests are also a part of the capitalist machine, and in these days a very important part. A Government committed to the improvement of capitalist profits can no more attack the vested interests of the distributors, wholesale and retail, however wasteful their methods may be, than it can attack the interests of the capitalist colliery owners or steel magnates. This way of reducing the wide margin between producers' and consumers' prices being ruled out, there is no course left open save the course of restriction—as the history of the milk and other marketing schemes very plainly shows. As long as capitalism is in the saddle, the horse cannot gallop. It will only be allowed to trot, for fear it may throw the rider if it be urged to a faster pace.

CHAPTER VI

CONCLUSION

THE foregoing chapters should have sufficed to bring out clearly at any rate one point. In only one of the five countries which I have attempted to study is any attempt being made to plan for the full use of the available resources of production in meeting the demands of human welfare. That country is, of course, the one Socialist country—the U.S.S.R. All the rest are pursuing policies which result either in a failure to use a substantial fraction of the resources available, or in their use for uneconomic and even positively anti-social ends.

The Soviet economy is planned for welfare—even though welfare, in the sense of a high standard of living, is for the citizens of the Soviet Union still some distance off. If they are poor, it is because they have not the technical means to produce more—save indeed to the extent to which aggressive armament by Germany and Japan is forcing the diversion of productive resources to defensive armament upon the Soviet Union. They are not poor because they are leaving resources deliberately unused, as the democratic capitalist countries are. The U.S.S.R. has no unemployment problem.

The German economy, and the Italian economy to a somewhat smaller extent, because Italians are easier going and less thorough than Germans, are planned for brigandage. If Germany has now relatively few unemployed, that is not because she has found them work in raising the common standard of life. Quite the contrary. The German people is continually adjured to tighten its belt, to do without this or that, in order that the country may be better armed for war. Exports that could be used to pay for imports which the people sorely need go to pay for war materials. Production is directed, under the Four Year Plan, not to raising the standard of life, but to lowering it, in order to promote economic self-sufficiency with a view to war. Only successful brigandage on a world-wide scale could make this sort of 'planning' pay, in any economic sense. Moreover, it is most unlikely that even the most successful brigandage imaginable could make it pay. German planned economy is profoundly uneconomic. It reproduces the anti-social character of the robber on a national scale that threatens to reduce all Western civilisation to ruin.

The American economy, on the other hand, is not planned at all—only tied together with bits of Government string, while the machinery of private capitalism is undergoing repair. The New Deal

CONCLUSION 251

was an attempt, not to plan industry, but to provide emergency relief and employment, and to rescue capitalist enterprises from bankruptcy in order to enable the profit-making machine to resume control. If it has at certain points been forced beyond this, so that the State cannot wholly draw back from the new obligations which it has assumed, this advance has been unintentional, and will be kept within the narrowest possible limits. Already the United States is well back on the road towards planless capitalism.

The British economy has been more lastingly, though much less extremely, affected by the crisis. For the British excursions into sectional planning seem mostly meant to be permanent. They embody a half-hearted attempt to make capitalism work better by putting the various branches of production under the collective control of the profit-makers. But the necessarily restrictive consequences of this policy are already provoking an outcry from consumers, and a demand for 'disinterested' control. Witness the recent report of the Milk Reorganisation Commission, which proposes that the producer-controlled Milk Marketing Board should be made subject to an impartial Milk Commission appointed by the State to represent the general interest. It is clear, however, that any such proposal will be fought hard by the profit-making interests. The Milk Report has already been roundly denounced by the National Farmers' Union. The public interest favours increased consumption, not higher profits.

What, then, are the morals to be drawn from these studies in the working of State intervention? Fundamentally, the main moral is that capitalism, by reason of its very nature, cannot plan, whereas Socialism can and must. Under Capitalism, the object of those who organise production is not the satisfaction of needs, but the appropriation of profits. They will therefore set out to employ the available resources only up to the point beyond which further employment means the prospect of a smaller return. Socialism, on the other hand, views the entire available supply of labour and other productive instruments solely as means to the satisfaction of human wants. Wants being limitless, in relation to the present means of satisfying them, it is clearly uneconomic to leave any usable resource unused, up to the point beyond which leisure, or amenity in the case of natural resources, has more power to satisfy wants than a farther supply of goods. Under Socialism there not only is not— there cannot be an unemployment problem.

It is true that even under capitalism the point at which the available resources are in full employment can on occasion be nearly approached. This can happen in a boom, though even booms nowadays are apt to fall a good way short of it. But

CONCLUSION

even if, during a boom, unemployment is reduced to a low level, under capitalist conditions this situation cannot last. The boom exists because capitalists, able to make high profits in the present and hoping for their continuance, are prepared to invest on a grand scale in new instruments of production. This rate of investment, however, can be maintained only on condition that consuming power and the will to consume continue to expand fast enough to take off the market at remunerative prices the additional goods which the new instruments are in a position to supply.

This, however, cannot happen; for capitalism so distributes purchasing power that, the further the boom goes, the greater the inequality of incomes becomes. This growing inequality leads to a disproportionate growth of savings, or in other words to a less than proportionate growth of the will to consume. Consumers' demand sooner or later falls behind the expanding power to produce.

As soon as this occurs, investment is bound to slacken off; for the prospect of future profit fades away. But the slackening of investment necessarily produces a crisis. Workers in the capital goods industries are discharged, and lose their incomes; and thereupon workers in other industries have to be discharged as well. Slump develops cumulatively, as it must when the total current expenditure (consumption *plus* investment) adds up to less than the total price at which the current amount of output can be profitably produced.

Capitalist booms are therefore inherently unstable. Nor can any amount of capitalist 'planning' give them stability. There is only one condition on which a capitalist economy can maintain 'full employment' for any length of time. This condition is that the State shall so act as to maintain the demand for the factors of production at the requisite level.

The State can do this by a policy of public works, accompanied by monetary expansion—or rather by the absence of monetary contraction if the State takes action to sustain a boom rather than to correct a slump after it has occurred. But public works are expensive. Even if they are financed largely by borrowing, they involve interest charges which fall on the taxpayers. No capitalist State except America has hitherto been persuaded to use public works policy on the really grand scale, although Sweden, with a much smaller problem to face, did deal with it along these lines in recent years, under a Socialist Government, with really significant success.

Expensiveness is not the only difficulty in the way of an effective public works policy. Under capitalism, the State has to seek out public works which will not compete with private enterprise; for otherwise it will be in danger of causing capitalist

CONCLUSION 255

recession instead of revival. But such works are bound to be largely 'uneconomic' from the capitalist point of view, however socially useful they may be. Capitalist Governments will therefore look askance at them, and as a rule pursue them only half-heartedly if at all. The necessity of avoiding competition with private capitalism made many of the public works attempted under the New Deal quite ludicrously wasteful. In many cases, the object was plainly to provide employment anyhow, rather than to put it to economic or even social use.

In fact, the only circumstances under which capitalism is compatible with full employment, for more than very brief periods of self-destructive boom, arise when capitalism is either actually at war, or getting ready for it so energetically as to be prepared to absorb all surplus labour either into the armed forces or into works of war production or supply. But this, too, is ruinous in the long run; for the huge wasteful expenditure on armaments, accompanied by large profits for the armament industries, depresses the standard of living and creates conditions of depression for the industries supplying ordinary consumers' demands.

For a time, however, capitalism can reduce unemployment to a low level by intensive preparation for war. It can do this only at the cost of piling up public debt, and being confronted with a major economic crisis as soon as the process of war preparation slackens off. Under these conditions, an aggressive capitalist Power can for a time find employment for its citizens, but only at a greatly depressed standard of life.

My final moral, then, is that unless we want to convert the world into armed camps of impoverished peoples, we must plan for plenty—that is, for increased consumption—in ways which are quite inconsistent with the retention of the capitalist system.

NOTE.—This book can be regarded as, in some sense, an introduction to my *Principles of Economic Planning*, in which its positive implications are worked out in much fuller detail.